Big Data Challenges

Anno Bunnik • Anthony Cawley • Michael Mulqueen • Andrej Zwitter
Editors

Big Data Challenges

Society, Security, Innovation and Ethics

Editors
Anno Bunnik
Media and Communication
Liverpool Hope University
Liverpool, United Kingdom

Anthony Cawley
Media and Communication
Liverpool Hope University
Liverpool, United Kingdom

Michael Mulqueen
Leicestershire Police
Leicester, United Kingdom

Andrej Zwitter
Faculty of Law
University of Groningen
Groningen, The Netherlands

ISBN 978-1-349-94884-0   ISBN 978-1-349-94885-7   (eBook)
DOI 10.1057/978-1-349-94885-7

Library of Congress Control Number: 2016936676

Printed on acid-free paper

This Palgrave Macmillan imprint is published by Springer Nature
The registered company is Macmillan Publishers Ltd. London

Acknowledgements

This book is one of several outcomes from a process that started with a meeting between academics from Liverpool Hope University and Globalisation Studies Groningen, University of Groningen, on a sunny day in the Netherlands in 2013. The common theme of the dialogue revolved around the wide range of challenges related to the advent of the Big Data age. Other academics and practitioners have since joined the network, and several of them have kindly contributed to this book. The International Network Observatory (INO), a consortium of Academic and Non-Academic Partners on Big Data, Global Strategy and Ethics, has been founded. More information on INO can be found on http://www.networkobservatory.org/

We would like to thank our institutions for facilitating the fruitful dialogue that resulted in this work, as well as all those who supported our work in any shape or form.

CONTENTS

NOTES ON CONTRIBUTORS

Anno Bunnik is a PhD research fellow at Liverpool Hope University. His doctoral dissertation assesses the implementation of Big Data by law enforcement agencies in the UK. His research interests include intelligence, law enforcement, national security, and counter-terrorism. Bunnik also publishes on contemporary security issues in the Middle East region, specifically Lebanon, Syria, and Iraq.

Anthony Cawley is a Lecturer in Media at Liverpool Hope University. His original research articles have appeared in Irish and international peer-reviewed journals. His research interests include media industry innovation, news framing of current affairs, online journalism, media history, and Big Data and media.

Bryce Evans is Senior Lecturer in History at Liverpool Hope University. A graduate of the University of Warwick and University College Dublin, he researches food security and modern British and Irish history.

David Lundie is a senior lecturer in the Faculty of Education at Liverpool Hope University. His research interests include digital ethics and the anthropology of data analytics. He has published on the impact of learning analytics, the relation between artificial intelligence and moral autonomy, and the relationship between education, safeguarding, and security. David also publishes on religion, values, and education.

Michael Mulqueen is a serving senior police officer actively engaged in strategic police initiatives to better sense, seize, and exploit the opportunities of digital intelligence and investigation through ethical innovation. He holds a PhD from University College Dublin, where he was a Government of Ireland Scholar. He previously was Professor of Media and Security Innovation at Liverpool Hope University, where he also served as founding Director of the Centre for Applied Research in Security Innovation and Head of the Department of Media and

ix

Communication. He was executive lead of the UK's Intelligence Futures Group, which was established by the Association of Chief Police Officers.

Philipp Olbrich is a PhD student in the Department of International Relations and International Organization at the University of Groningen. Prior to that, he was a researcher at the Austrian Institute for International Affairs in Vienna. His doctoral dissertation focuses on the use of commercial satellite imagery by non-state actors in the context of international security. His broader research interests concern the nexus of international security and technology, materialist approaches in international relations, and the conflict on the Korean peninsula.

David Reid is Senior Lecturer in Computing at Liverpool Hope University. Having attained his PhD in 1995, on research in the fields of intelligent agent systems and adapted hypertext systems, he joined a newly formed group at Liverpool University, dedicated to developing and promoting innovative technological solutions for local businesses. After implementing the first electronic shopping mall in the UK, Reid spent eight years providing technical leadership on many Internet and Intranet projects, including novel biometric data storage and analysis. His current research interests include web-based biometric security, agent-based systems, genetic programming, and artificial intelligence.

Julian Richards holds a PhD in Political Violence from Cambridge University in 1993. He subsequently worked for Government Communications Headquarters in the UK for a number of years, before returning to academic life and co-founding the Centre for Security and Intelligence Studies at the University of Buckingham in 2008, where he leads a number of postgraduate programmes.

Ian Stanier has nearly 25 years' experience in Law Enforcement Intelligence, including within two large metropolitan police forces and a secondment to the National Offender Management Service. He received a doctorate from London Metropolitan University, where he studied information-sharing pathologies and police intelligence failures. His overt and covert intelligence work has seen him deployed nationally and internationally. He has taught various intelligence-related subjects at the College of Policing and is responsible for covert units within his current organisation. He specialises in intelligence-failure pathologies, prisoner debriefing, covert policing, and intelligence collection within prison establishments. He has worked with UK universities to increase academic provision for law enforcement intelligence professionals.

Nina Witjes is a research fellow at the Austrian Institute for International Affairs in Vienna and a scientific associate at Munich Center for Technology in Society (MCTS), Research Group on Innovation. Witjes is finalising her doctoral dissertation at the Technical University Munich on 'The Co-Production of Science, Technology and International Politics'. Her research interests revolve around science, technology and global affairs, the European Space Agency and the nexus of satellite technologies and security policy as well as large technological infrastructures in the context of European Integration.

Andrej Zwitter holds the Nederlands Genootschap voor Internationale Zaken (NGIZ) Chair in International Relations at the Faculty of Law, the University of Groningen, and is also an honorary senior research fellow at the Liverpool Hope University. In his function as NGIZ-Chair, he heads the Political Sciences section at the Department of Legal Theory. His research foci include ethics in international politics and law, the ethics of Big Data, state-of-emergency politics, as well as law and politics of humanitarian action.

LIST OF FIGURES

CHAPTER 1

Introduction to Big Data Challenges

Anno Bunnik, Anthony Cawley, Michael Mulqueen, and Andrej Zwitter

Abstract This chapter introduces the rationale for the book. It explains why Big Data is one of the most prominent challenges of our time, with far-reaching implications for society and security. It sets out why the tension, and interaction, between innovation and ethics is at the forefront of the various challenges of Big Data. It clarifies the division of the book into Part I, 'Between Mathematics and Philosophy', and Part II on 'Implications for Security'. Each chapter is also briefly introduced to the reader.

Keywords Introduction • Big Data • Security • Society • Innovation • Ethics

This book unravels implications for society and security of a seismic shift in science, engineering, and computing. Driving the shift is 'Big Data', a term that loosely refers to remarkable advances in computational processing power, information storage, and clever software programmes. Whilst there is no universal definition of Big Data, it can be understood as referring to vast digital data sets that often capture very personal information of citizens and consumers. Examples would include Google searches, WhatsApp messages, or financial transaction flows by Walmart's clientele.

A. Bunnik (✉) • A. Cawley • M. Mulqueen • A. Zwitter
Department of Media and Communication, Liverpool Hope University, Liverpool, UK

© The Editor(s) (if applicable) and The Author(s) 2016   1
A. Bunnik et al. (eds.), *Big Data Challenges*,
DOI 10.1057/978-1-349-94885-7_1

These data sets are increasingly recognised as a source to be harvested, aggregated, and analysed by, first and foremost, the private sector—corporate powerhouses have emerged in recent years that have adopted a business model largely on the promise of Big Data. Big Data's significance may lie not only in the tsunami of information and the insights it is helping to gather, but in how it transforms the essence of decision-making and enables organisations to adapt to a radically altered landscape.

The public sector, academia, and non-governmental organisations (NGOs) are increasingly recognising Big Data's potential as well. The challenges that Big Data poses for these sectors are perhaps more complex and less well researched than developments in the corporate world. Innovation, after all, is part of the DNA of capitalism, but is less well embedded within government agencies. The age of Big Data, however, presents an opportunity to these actors to embrace data-driven innovation and utilise the banks of information that are available to them to make better sense of the world around them. But how can and should governments, academics, and NGOs adopt Big Data in a sustainable manner?

This volume emerged as a response to these timely issues and has a strong focus on the interplay between *society* and *security* and between *ethics* and *innovation*. It will operate from the perspective that Big Data prompts manifold opportunities for innovation and risk-management. Practically, Big Data opens up scarcely imagined challenges for practitioners working in security, intelligence, and law enforcement. Simultaneously, it promises game-changing progress in cost-effective technologies and processes to enable agencies to operate with unprecedented efficiency and productivity. In relation to society and security, Big Data will be unpacked as a triptych of scientific, corporate, and societal concern, albeit one in which the parts are currently dangerously disconnected from the whole.

Advances in private and public laboratories are taking place largely removed from the scrutiny of the societal communities (artistic, political, and legal) that traditionally interpret the implications of radical turns in technology for humanity. Indeed, the news media, it will be argued, has shown scarce capacity to interrogate Big Data developments on behalf of the citizens who depend upon it for translation of important events. Where it has—as in the recent revelations in the Edward Snowden affair—the unintended cost in terms of blowback on states can be measured by compromised life-saving intelligence as well as jobs lost.

This book will, therefore, argue that the disconnection is both a hindrance to innovation for the many and a seam through which ethically dubious and practically dangerous developments can take place. The text will conclude by calling for a new methodological approach amongst scholars and 'real world' practitioners alike: the moment has arrived for a previously unimagined blurring of hard and social sciences to effect sustainable innovation that is ethically informed. This development can be achieved only by weaving together, in imaginative ways, knowledge and understanding from the sciences, humanities, and arts.

More broadly, security and law enforcement organisations internationally have reported to us serious concerns for corporate risk management arising from mining and analysing data. One aspect of this problem is how the traditional 'signals to noise' issue of useless/crucial information is reaching an unprecedented scale. Such organisations are hungry for solutions to help them to carry emerging data risk. In these communities, we are seeing a real interest in smart technological solutions but equally in realistic policy limitations for information operations and the management of political and media expectations, especially when things go wrong.

Bibliometric data gathered by the authors suggests that limited ethical discussions have taken place around the security threats posed by Big Data and communication aggregation. The result may be unwanted consequences for the state, business, and individual human rights. Our research also indicates weak journalistic interrogation of Big-Data-based evidence linked to negative consequences for national economic security. Whilst a plurality of legal approaches have been reported from around the world, the one point of consensus appears to be that legislation is structurally unable to keep pace with rapid advances in technology. Experimental work carried out by colleagues in collaboration with Cornell University suggests that privacy disclosure decisions have a highly unstable value at a personal level, meaning that users' decisions are heavily influenced by emotion, calling into question the role of rational consent, at the core of much privacy-related legislation to date.

In these and many other ways, governments are lagging behind the corporate sector in their consideration of the uses, analyses, and ethics of aggregating large data-sets to create an increasingly fine-grained picture of individual and group activities. The limited contact among the technical, entrepreneurial, legislative, and academic weakens the societal scope to regulate and interpret the developments associated with Big Data. This volume serves as much as an academic interdisciplinary response to a pressing real-world problem as it is a call to action to those working to keep us safe and secure.

ORGANISATION OF THE BOOK

The book is divided into two parts. Part I consists of conceptual explorations of Big Data through various mathematic and/or philosophical lenses. These chapters approach the topic with specific reference to the domains of computer science, philosophy of information, ethics, and media studies. These particular prisms were carefully selected to provide a deeper understanding of the radical change presented through Big Data. Part II takes a more empirical turn, and deals with Big Data's ramifications on security, intelligence, and law enforcement in particular. How are these communities looking to embed Big Data in their organisations and practices? And does it indeed provide the innovation that they seek so as to respond to the contemporary threats of an increasingly digital and global world?

Part I: Between Mathematics and Philosophy

Chapter 2 traces the origins of Big Data by providing a brief history of data science and the 'civil war' between statisticians and machine learners. David Reid argues here that the impact of data now signifies a paradigm shift in the history of humanity as a machine rather than humankind's being able to classify the world around us—a development often understood as machine learning. The reader is also treated to a discussion of the N = all debate, deep learning, and what this all means for society.

In Chap. 3, Andrej Zwitter emphasises the radical departure that the Big Data age signifies for researchers, corporates, and public bodies alike. The argument is presented that the nature of Big Data and the means of analysis raise their own specific ethical problems that nowadays go beyond the privacy consideration of the individual. Instead, these changes raise questions about the privacy of communities against the collecting and tracking of group and network data, the security from manipulation, and education for appropriate internet use. Do our ethical frameworks still fit the Big Data age? The author concludes that we might need to redevelop individualistic ethical norms to match a network logic of power and responsibility.

Following from computer science and ethics, the Chap. 4 builds on some of the topics and questions raised earlier through the philosophical assumptions that have governed the evolution of online networks. These assumptions, drawn from the philosophy of mathematics, carry with them their own definitions of knowledge, intelligence, and security, which are not always compatible with the working definitions in either the intelligence community or the wider human domain. Drawing on a few practical examples, David Lundie examines some of the critical incidents that can result from this mismatch of design and purpose, and proposes an approach to values in design that can mitigate these concerns.

Chapter 5 of Part I deals with the role of news media in the age of Big Data and how this role relates to some of the ontological debates in this field: What is the core purpose of news and should news be classed primarily as a public good or a product? Anthony Cawley explains how Big Data underpins the emergence of data journalism, and he argues that an increasingly data-driven world is amongst the expanding list of social and technological complexities that the news media is expected to explain to the public. A case study of innovation in news media in Ireland considers some of these questions in more detail.

Part II: Implications for Security

Part II deals with the wider ramifications of Big Data for security and society. The concept of security here has a focus on the state, but goes beyond the realm of national security. Law enforcement, counter-terrorism, and food security are equally affected by Big Data and have, therefore, been addressed in this book. How are the agencies mandated with these tasks adapting their strategies, tactics, and operations to make full use of the innovation that Big Data presents? And what are the core challenges that need to be overcome to ensure these changes will prove to be effective as well as legitimate and sustainable?

Chapter 6, by Michael Mulqueen, opens this section on the security implications of Big Data. To what extent should state agencies make decisions on the basis of no other evidence than algorithmic sorting of messy, raw data? And how do these agencies marry innovation with ethics in order to prevent blowback from the media and public? This chapter raises pertinent ethical problems and addresses the need for professional ethics in organisations working on security. It is argued that decisions to deploy Big Data are being made in the absence of any systematic epistemology or methodology to track and manage the influences of human intuition and social processes on that action.

In Chap. 7, Julian Richards argues that Edward Snowden's revelations about the nature and scale of data collection by American and British intelligence agencies added a new dimension to a debate already underway about the transformation of intelligence-gathering in an age of Big Data. Snowden's revelations provided the bow-wave of a fundamentally critical and anti-state stance on the intelligence questions in hand. Such a critical stance is reflected in much of the academic literature about Big Data. In this chapter, such concerns are critically appraised. It is concluded that the slippery and sometimes deliberate mutation in public discourse of large-scale collection of data into 'mass surveillance' is misleading and unhelpful.

Chapter 8 explores the ramifications of Big Data for the contemporary challenges of countering terrorism, extremism, and radicalisation. Given the recent rise of jihadists and other extremists in the Middle East and Europe, how do state agencies respond to this challenge through Big Data? This chapter critically engages with questions such as the extent to which Big Data can inform us of future terrorist attacks, the prevention of radicalisation, and the role of the private sector and NGOs. The author, Anno Bunnik, argues here that academics and subject matter experts need to be involved in this process to better understand the relationship between extremism, radicalisation, and terrorism.

Chapter 9 offers an overview of primary Big Data sets that are 'owned' by or formally accessible to UK law enforcement. It examines, through the lens of practitioners, how Big Data is utilised in mitigating identified or anticipated harm to individuals and communities. It outlines accompanying oversight and governance arrangements that provide scrutiny, enhanced public accountability, and legitimacy, and guards the legality of data management. Ian Stanier explores the key organisational, technological, ethical, and cultural challenges faced by law enforcement as it seeks to exploit Big Data when discharging its legal responsibilities in safeguarding communities, reducing crime, and addressing anti-social behaviour.

Chapter 10 takes a closer look at the millions of square kilometres of high-resolution satellite imagery produced daily and which pose novel opportunities and challenges for state as well as non-state actors. It addresses the techno-political development of Earth observation, the changing ways of knowledge production, and the policy impact and governance of geospatial Big Data. Following this trichotomy, Philipp Olbrich and Nina Witjes outline how the satellite imagery community contributes to the formation of a specific sociotechnical imaginary of geospatial Big Data. The two notions most prevalent in the accounts of satellite imagery providers, government officials, and imagery analysts are a sense of condensed temporality and increasing transparency.

Chapter 11, by Bryce Evans, focuses on advancement of food security through better knowledge of novel ecosystem data. It is argued that leveraging Big Data can improve food security by reducing delays in the gathering, processing, and diffusion of information, allowing for more efficient, analytically-informed decision-making. In these ways, Big Data would form an essential part of the toolkit of established assessments used to identify food insecure populations, such as the World Food Programme's Vulnerability Analysis and Mapping. The use of Big Data, therefore, has the potential to bolster food security and, in some contexts, to take its place as the centrepiece of new initiatives to combat hunger.

PART I

Between Mathematics and Philosophy

CHAPTER 2

Man vs. Machine: The Battle for the Soul of Data Science

David Reid

Abstract David Reid asks if data science is just a trendy rebadging of statistics, or whether it is something fundamentally new. The chapter describes how two camps—data scientists and statisticians—are battling for the 'soul' of data science. The essence of this fight is the argument for and against the concept of 'automated reasoning'. Just as the wheel allowed mankind to physically carry far greater loads, could another technology—automated reasoning—enable people to share intellectual burdens? Advances in Artificial Intelligence using Big Data could mean people are no longer the sole agents of genuine discovery and may soon share this special attribute with genuinely intelligent and inventive machines.

Keywords Big Data • Algorithms • Data science • Statistics • Artificial intelligence • Machine learning • Automated reasoning • Human intelligence

THE MACHINE AS DATA SCIENTIST

Throughout history, mankind has sought significance in numbers. Science, art and religion have all used numbers as the agent to validate a particular view of the world and to justify or refute suppositions. Interpreting meaning

D. Reid (✉)
Department of Mathematics and Computer Science,
Liverpool Hope University, Liverpool, UK

© The Editor(s) (if applicable) and The Author(s) 2016   11
A. Bunnik et al. (eds.), *Big Data Challenges*,
DOI 10.1057/978-1-349-94885-7_2

in quantifiable data has always equated to power in society. Knowledge acquisition involves complex cognitive processes: perception, communication and reasoning, always perceived as distinctly human qualities. At the dawn of the technological age, the influence of numbers cannot be underestimated. Numbers are the agent that delineates, defines and categorises all of us. Thus far in history, it is people who had dominion over numbers. People looked for the patterns, people interpret these patterns and people build testable models of our world.

This situation may be about to change. Machine learning has recently been developing so rapidly that soon machines may be able to independently construct correlations, draw inferences about the significance of events and learn from data taken directly from the real world. We may be on the brink of an age where, for the first time in history, that mastery over the meaning of numbers is taken from mankind and is given to machines.

The people traditionally charged with gleaning understanding from data are statisticians. The fledgling discipline of data science is largely based on the pioneer statistics developed in the late nineteenth century. Many statisticians see data science as merely the trendy rebranding of what they have been doing for decades. They see the data that scientists are advocating as a simple redefinition of existing statistical nomenclature, leading to many conflicts between the two major influences in the new discipline of data science: the computer scientist/machine learners and the statisticians. This antipathy has existed since the term 'Data Science' was coined in 1974 by Peter Naur (1974), but the roots of the schizophrenic nature of data science go back even further, to 1962 when John W. Tukey (a statistician) wrote about data analysis (Tukey 1962):

> For a long time I thought I was a statistician, interested in inferences from the particular to the general. But as I have watched mathematical statistics evolve, I have had cause to wonder and doubt ... I have come to feel that my central interest is in data analysis ... data analysis is intrinsically an empirical science not mathematics.

So is data science merely a reinvention of statistics, or is it something new, and, more important, do humans (statisticians) need to be at the core of the discipline? Both statisticians and advocates of machine learning approach their disciplines in a similar manner. They formulate a hypothesis; gather data; tidy the data; analyse data; and transform the data into useful information in order to communicate findings. However, the emphasis given to each of these steps and the different approaches employed in each step create a clear distinction between the two camps.

Statistics, concerned with the mechanics of how data is collected, is primarily (but not wholly) focused on gathering data.. The sampling method used and design of experiment are critical. Supporters of machine learning take a more pragmatic approach. The data is out there; can we do anything with it?

Tidying the data so that we can proceed to the next step of analysis is important in both disciplines. If we have a well-formed experiment with a clearly defined hypothesis, as is likely in statistics, then relatively little cleaning is needed. The data is almost always homogenous. However, if the data has been pulled from a number of sources, and the data is of many different types that may have had nothing to do with the original experiment, as is likely in machine learning, then the data will require a great deal of wrangling to get it into a state ready for processing and analysis.

Data analysis often involves the complementary processes of visualisation and modelling. These processes are complementary because visualisation tends to rely on human interpretation, whereas modelling is essentially taking an abstraction of the real worlds and trying to reproduce that abstraction (often inside a machine). Visualisation may throw up new discoveries, whereas modelling will only tell one whether the model is working. Statisticians like models. Statistics is often about using the right model, which initially involves finding the correct probability distribution function (normal, uniform, Caucy, t, F, Chi-Square, exponential, Weibull, Birnbaum-Suanders, Tukey-Lambda and so on) to best fit the data. Models confirm hypotheses. Distribution functions provide the building blocks for those models. Machine learners also use models, but models for machine learners fulfil a slightly different role. Machine learning is a more engineered approach in that scientists creating machine learning systems are primarily concerned with how a robust system can be built that can react to different shapes of data. In this sense, it is only the machine's internal, implicit and, to a large extent, unknown conceptualisation of the data that is considered important for the overall functioning of the system.

When communicating the data, one needs to ask the question of to whom are you communicating your findings? Statisticians generally use their findings to impart insights to other humans. Machine learners may do this, but they may also use these insights to feed their results into other automated reasoning systems.

However, it is the first act—the formulation of a hypothesis—that gives rise to the starkest distinction between statisticians and proponents of machine learning. Statistics claim that a human-generated hypothesis is vital to perform science, whilst machine learners claim that, if the data set is large enough, the road to understanding cause and effect can be derived entirely through the calculation of correlation.

In general, statistics is concerned with analysing primary (experimental) data that has been explicitly collected to check a specific hypothesis. In this sense, statistics is top down, testing hypotheses by using primary observation whereas machine learning is often concerned with analysing secondary (observational) data that has been collected for other purposes, so, in this sense, machine learning is bottom-up, trying to fit messy data into a workable system (Tukey 1980).

Vasant Dhar, professor in New York University's Stern School of Business and Director of its Center for Business Analytics, articulated the difference in focus between statisticians and machine learners most clearly. He says it is the difference between explaining and predicting (Dhar 2013). Statistics has been generally used as a way of explaining some phenomenon by extracting interesting patterns from individual data sets with well-formulated queries. Machine learning, on the other hand, aims to discover and extract actionable knowledge from the data. A big motivation for machine learning is to use knowledge to *continually* refine decisions and predictions. As such, machine learning is more dynamic and immediate than statistics in that it is not just concerned with using past data on a *static* model to make predictions.

Vasant Dhar also takes the viewpoint that data science, using machine learning, is a genuine departure from statistics in that correlation, on its own, is proof. The automated correlations are just as important (or more so) than human-derived hypotheses.

THE CASE AGAINST AUTOMATED REASONING

Many people (Mayer-Schönberger and Cukier 2013) have stated that automated reasoning or hypothesis generation means giving up on knowing the causes, because access to vast quantities of data can seduce researchers into making incorrect assumptions. Researchers, particularly automated ones, can often assume the number of observations in the sample is equal to everybody out there. This assumption is often called N = All, and is particularly problematic for machine-learning systems trying to automatically derive hypotheses from data because often the data needs to be simplified. It is all too easy to swamp even the most sophisticated machine-learning algorithm with massive amounts of variables, permutations of relationships between variables and subjects, or insignificant/irrelevant data. Often this swamping occurs whilst 'cleaning' the data. How do automated systems know what is good data and what is 'noise' when cleaning the data? How do they know they are not junking important data?

It is also important to remember who is part of the sample. It could be that the population from which one is getting the data is a significant subset of N and that N can be self-selecting. This idea is perhaps best illustrated by Gavin Jackson (Jackson 2014) on his post about the dating website OkCupid in his blog, 'Damned Lies and Statistics'. His analysis of OkCupid data shows that men consistently message significantly younger women than the youngest allowable match listed on their profile. This implies:

a) that men prefer significantly younger women and
b) that men are liars.

It would be easy to imagine a machine-learning algorithm arriving at these two conclusions from this set of data. However, OkCupid has a significantly larger number of younger women in its database than older women (there are six times more 22-year-olds than 48-year-olds). So whilst the implication may be true in general, it may be that older men more often message younger women simply because there are more of them in OkCupid's database.

If N = All, N may also be just one. I call this the Three Musketeers' dilemma or the All-for-One-and-One-for-All dilemma. It is possible to gather vast amounts of data (Big Data) from an individual subject, particularly in the health field, where a great deal of genomic and biometric data may be collected from an individual over a short period of time. In this case, it is possible to model an individual person, but it may be a mistake, however tempting, to infer things about the larger population given this small sample.

The issues above are major barriers to automated reasoning, but do we have to give up on knowing the causes of specific phenomena because we derive correlations in large data sets? It could be argued that reasoning is reasoning, whether it is automated or not, and, if reasoning can be followed, then the causes of a result can be ascertained by deduction.

THE CASE FOR AUTOMATED REASONING

The present champion for machine learning is the Deep Belief Network (DBN), an old idea with a modern twist. Based on traditional neural network architectures dating from the 1980s, DBNs were developed and promoted by Geoffrey Hinton and Ruslan Salakhutdinov (2006). They demonstrated how a system can learn from data by viewing the data from different perspectives. Such systems have increased massively in capability in recent times because of the sheer quantity and variety of data available to them. Such systems can cross-correlate data from many different sources to create an internal cognitive model and automatically determine the key features of that model. The automated derivation of key features provides the most excitement in machine learning at the moment. This function is also at the hub of the conflict between the statisticians and advocates of machine learning. The machine learners, with a pragmatic engineering viewpoint, do not care how this internal cognitive model works but are just interested in whether it works. The statisticians take a more traditionally scientific viewpoint and say that the most efficient way is complete understanding, which would ultimately lead to a manually handcrafted solution based on the most appropriate distribution model.

This is analogous to the classic black box versus white box testing choice in software engineering. Whereas white box testing requires the user to know the programming and implementation details, in black box testing, the tester does not know which internal structure, design, or implementation of the item is being tested.

In short, proponents of machine learning claim that one can build, or teach, a DBN that not only does not require the user to know the inner workings of the system, but also does not require the user to have subject knowledge at all. However, the strongest argument for automated hypotheses is that DBNs already exist that are starting to automatically derive meaning from data independently from humans.

THE EVIDENCE OF AUTOMATED REASONING

The Google Brain project, using a cluster of 16,000 computers, successfully trained itself to recognise cats based on 10 million digital images taken from YouTube videos (Le et al. 2013). The significant thing about this project is that, unlike with past expert systems, no complex rules were applied, no expert knowledge was encoded, and no pre-processing took place. The system learnt what a cat looked like by being presented, independent of any human assistance, with millions of pictures of cats. Google then went on to use the same techniques to build an 800-machine speech recognition system that was trained for five and produced the biggest single improvement in word error rate for English in 20 years of speech research. The same methods were then used to automatically label (or caption) objects in *any* picture. The system achieved an error rate of less than 7%, approximately the same rate as a human identifying an object in a picture.

The Watson Supercomputer beat the best human competitors on the TV quiz show 'Jeopardy' in 2011. Watson required complex speech analysis not only to understand the question, but also to formulate a sensible response from general knowledge. Like Google's system, Watson then evolved to be used in other areas. It is now employed in drug-trial matching at the Mayo Clinic; it is a chef, creating original written recipes; it diagnoses lung cancer in the Memorial Sloan Kettering Cancer Center; and it is used by Elemental Path as a chatterbot to provide conversations for children's toys (Watson 2015).

Similar systems use DBNs in image recognition to diagnose cancer cells in the laboratory. Some systems now perform better than human pathologists. Recently, a system developed at Stanford discovered that the cells around a cancerous cell also provide markers for disease. This discovery is something that was completely unexpected by trained pathologists but was found by the computer alone. Companies are now building systems that can make diagnoses despite the company's not employing any medical personnel (Enlitic 2015).

Siri, Google and Cortana have all used DBNs to significantly improve their speech recognition systems. A team from Microsoft wrote a program for a system that can perform real-time translation of English into Mandarin Chinese and vice versa. Whilst it is far from perfect, it is good enough for basic translation. One of the most significant things about this system, however, is that nobody on the team that produced the system could speak Mandarin (Dahl et al. 2011). A DBN read Chinese handwritten texts and translate them into English; again, the DBN was programmed by a team that did not understand Chinese (Graves and Schmidhuber 2009)

In 2013, DeepMind (now owned by Google) produced a reinforcement-learning algorithm that allowed a computer to learn to play any Atari 2600 video game. The system used a simple learning reward algorithm (based on high score) and raw pixel input to independently learn to play seven different types of computer game (Mnih et al. 2015a). No one on the team told the system how to play any of the games it mastered.

DBNs are being used on robotics and self-drive cars. Both Google and Nvidia (Lari and Douma 2014) use DBNs to distinguish among different kinds of vehicles. Such cars have driven millions of miles without incident and are just starting to come onto our streets (Wakefield 2015). The rules for driving are learnt and derived, not coded.

What is different from the past is that all of these various fields—robotics, natural language processing, speech recognition, image recognition machine translation, and so on—are being developed through *one* set of machine-learning techniques—DBNs. Suddenly, machine learning is evolving at an accelerated rate.

This acceleration is likely to increase as advances in hardware support the functional substrate on which DBNs operate. IBM is developing a new generation of neurosynaptic chips (the SyNapse chip) that will surpass the processing capability of anything we have seen so far (Modha 2015). Google and NASA have set up the Quantum Artificial Intelligence Laboratory (QuAIL). Google are set to release their own quantum computers for DBNs (Google have been working with D-Wave quantum computer manufacturer since 2009). Memristor research and neuromorphic computing platforms, such as SP9 of the Human Brain Project (based on the SpiNNaker chip) (Furber 2015), are all technologies that are suited, to a lesser or greater degree, to DBNs.

A perfect storm of Big Data and exotic processing techniques has the potential to create DBNs that greatly surpass what was possible only a few years ago. The challenge in the near future will be to improve machine learning so that machines can learn without vast quantities of Big Data and that this learning is generalisable.

THE CONSEQUENCES OF AUTOMATED REASONING

If DBNs do fulfil even some of their potential, then the significance for data science and society is vast. The technologies outlined above mean that computers will be able to recognise images, read, speak, listen, play computer games and drive. The types of jobs computers can do will be vastly expanded. Deloitte and the University of Oxford predicted that 10 million unskilled jobs could be taken over by robots (Smith 2014). University of Oxford researchers Carl Benedict Frey and Michael Osborne estimated that 47% of US jobs could be automated and taken over by computers by 2033 (Frey and Osborne 2013). Thirty-five percent of UK jobs are at high risk from automation over the next two decades. If you earn less than £30,000 per year and you work in office or in administrative support, sales and services, transportation, construction extraction, or manufacturing, your job is particularly under threat. Out of a working population of 30 million, it is estimated that machine learning using Big Data could make 10.5 million jobs—about one-third of the workforce—redundant in the next 10-20 years.

White collar jobs that deal with any type of data processing or classification will be immediately under threat. Historically, the jobs that have been most highly prized and so far relatively untouched by changes in technology are in the professions. Doctors, lawyers, educators, researchers, journalists and architects are all threatened by machine learning. In all of these fields, researchers have shown how, by linking Big Data with machine learning, the cognitive processes involved in each of these jobs can be automated.

The USA, Russia, China and the UK are all working on autonomous weapons platforms. Noel Sharkey points out that advances in technology are so rapid that time for debate may be running out. Difficult questions about the legal and ethical implications of the use of such autonomous systems in warfare are yet to be answered, whilst at the same time development of such weapons increases unabated (Sharkey 2008).

In the so-called 'Flash Crash' in 2010, 10% was wiped off the stock market in a matter of minutes. This loss was fuelled by high frequency trading firms using automated tools. Automated orders can trigger extreme price swings. The interaction of these automatic orders with other high-frequency automated software means that liquidity can quickly be eroded. There is an incomplete understanding of the mechanics of how commodities in stock markets and derivatives markets interact. Should we just trust the DBNs to behave sensibly in all situations?

Stephen Hawking recently warned about the threat to humanity from machine learning and points out there is little serious research devoted to these issues outside non-profit institutes, such as the Cambridge Centre for the Study of Existential Risk, the Future of Humanity Institute, the Machine Intelligence Research Institute and the Future Life Institute. The potential benefits, and the potential risks, are colossal:

everything that civilisation has to offer is a product of human intelligence; we cannot predict what we might achieve when this intelligence is magnified by the tools that AI may provide, but the eradication of war, disease, and poverty would be high on anyone's list. Success in creating AI would be the biggest event in human history. (Hawking 2014)

Putting the Human Back into the Reasoning Loop

It may be that the best way to achieve a robust system is to handcraft some of the statistician's models and to incorporate these models into the DBNs. In this way, the 'common sense' of the human may augment the knowledge automatically derived by correlation in the machine. Some of the best DBNs are pre-trained or coached in order to teach the system more efficiently to perform a specific task. Recent reinforcement models for robotics have done this (Mnih et al. 2015b). Researchers from Pierre and Marie Curie University and the University of Wyoming have created a four-legged robot that can dynamically adapt its gait to compensate for injury in any of its limbs (Culley et al. 2015). Their important modification is the selection, by humans, of the predefined walking behaviours. In this way, the DBN is helped by human intervention. Its decisions are, therefore, coloured by our hand.

An additional benefit to this technique is that, by including in the system sets of strategies and models chosen by humans, we may be providing at least a minimal set of restraints on the system—a safety valve. At first sight, such restraint seems to go against the philosophy of DBN research, which gives full autonomy to the machine. Traditional DBNs autonomously choose features, parameters and models. However, future machines may learn better if humans challenge them by asking why they are taking a particular course of action and question the system about other alternatives. If we imbue in the machine the statistician's requirement to understand the function of the models it uses, we may build far more robust and sensible systems.

It may also be possible for such machines to learn from each other and, thus, pass on human-derived knowledge. If we are to build better automated systems, we may need to make those systems more accountable. We may need machines to work more like statisticians. As the barrier between the computer and the outside real world is lessened, machines will interact with us in much more immediate, influential and unexpected ways. The next challenge may be to interact with DBNs in a far more intimate way by including what we know about the world so that the DBN challenges its own internal assumptions.

As Marshal McLuhan argued, 'We become what we behold. We shape our tools and then our tools shape us' (Culkin 1967). Although he was thinking more of books and television, his concept applies perfectly to machine learning and data science. Development of machine learning and data science may ultimately depend on ideas from the amalgam of both man and machine.

REFERENCES

Culkin, J. (1967). A schoolman's guide to Marshall McLuhan. *Saturday Review*, pp. 51–53, 71–72

Culley, A., Clune, J., Tarapore, D., & Mouret, J.-B. (2015). Robots that can adapt like animals. *Nature, 521*(7553), 503–507.

Dahl, G. E., Yu, D., Deng, L., & Acero, A. (2011). *Large vocabulary continuous speech recognition with context-dependant DBN-HMMS.* International Conference on Acoustics, Speech and Signal Processing (ICASSP), IEEE (pp. 4688–4691).

Dhar, V. (2013). Data science and prediction. *Communications of the ACM, 56*(12), 64–73.

Enlitic. (2015). A modern machine learning company dedicated to revolutionising diagnostic healthcare. Retrieved July 14, 2015, from http://www.enlitic.com/

Frey, C. B., & Osborne, M. (2013). *The future of employment: How susceptible are jobs to computerisation?* Oxford University Programme on the Impact of Future Technologies Machine and Employment Workshop.

Furber, S. (2015). The Human Brain Project. Retrieved July 14, 2015, from https://www.humanbrainproject.eu/en_GB

Graves, A., & Schmidhuber, J. (2009). Offline handwriting recognition with multidimensional recurrent neural networks. In Y. Bengio and D. Schuurmans and J.D. Lafferty and C.K.I. Williams(Eds.), *Advances in Neural Information Processing Systems 22 (NIPS 2009)* (pp. 545–552). Cambridge, MA: MIT Press.

Hawking, S. (2014). Stephen Hawking warns AI could end mankind. *BBC Report.* Retrieved July 14, 2015, from http://www.bbc.co.uk/news/technology-30290540

Hinton, G. E., & Salakhutdinov, R. R. (2006). Reducing the dimensionality of data with neural networks. *Science, 313*(5786), 504–507.

Jackson, G. (2014). Big Data: When N doesn't equal all. Retrieved July 14, 2015,fromhttp://blogs.ft.com/ftdata/2014/08/04/big-data-when-n-doesnt-equal-all

Lari, A., & Douma, F. (2014). *Self-driving vehicles: Current status of autonomous vehicle development and Minnesota policy implications.* Preliminary White Paper, Minnesota Journal of Law, Science and Technology.

Le, Q. V., Ranzato, M. A., Monga, R., Devin, M., Chen, K., Corrado, G. S., et al. (2013). *Building high-level features using large scale unsupervised learning.* 29th International Conference in Machine Learning, Edinburgh.

Mayer-Schönberger, V., & Cukier, K. (2013). *Big Data: A revolution that will transform how we live, work and think.* Boston, MA: Houghton Mifflin Harcourt. ISBN 10: 1848547900.

Mnih, V., Kavukcuoglu, K., Silver, D., Graves, A., Antonoglou, I., Wierstra, D., et al. (2015a). *Playing Atari with deep reinforcement learning.* Technical Report: DeepMind Technologies, arXiv:1312.5602.

Mnih, V., Kavukcuoglu, K., Silver, D., Rusu, A. A., Veness, J., Bellemare, M. G., et al. (2015b). Human-level control through deep reinforcement learning. *Nature, 518*(7540), 529–533.

Modha, D. S. (2015). Introducing a brain-inspired computer: TrueNorth's neurons to revolutionize system architecture. Retrieved July 14, 2015, from http://www.research.ibm.com/articles/brain-chip.shtml

Naur, P. (1974). *Concise survey of computer methods.* New York: Petrocelli Books. ISBN 10: 0884053148.

Sharkey, N. (2008). Computer science: The ethical frontiers of robotics. *Science, 322*(5909), 1800–1801.

Smith, M. (2014). One-third of jobs in the UK at risk from automation. Retrieved July 14, 2015, from http://www2.deloitte.com/uk/en/pages/press-releases/articles/deloitte-one-third-of-jobs-in-the-uk-at-risk-from-automation.html

Tukey, J. W. (1962). The future of data analysis. *The Annals of Mathematical Statistics, 33*(1).

Tukey, J. W. (1980). We need both exploratory and confirmatory. *The American Statistician, 34*(1), 23–25.

Wakefield, J. (2015). Driverless car review launched by UK government. *BBC Report.* Retrieved July 14, 2015, from http://www.bbc.co.uk/news/technology-31364441

Watson. (2015). Say hello to Watson. Retrieved July 14, 2015, from http://www.ibm.com/smarterplanet/us/en/ibmwatson/

CHAPTER 3

The Network Effect on Ethics in the Big Data Age

Andrej Zwitter

Abstract This chapter emphasises the radical departure that the Big Data age signifies for researchers, corporates, and public bodies alike. It argues that the nature of Big Data and the means of analysis raise their own specific ethical problems that nowadays go beyond the privacy consideration of the individual. Instead, these changes raise questions about the privacy of communities against the collecting and tracking of group and network data, the security from manipulation, and education for appropriate internet use. The chapter reflects on whether our ethical frameworks still match the Big Data age. It concludes that we might need to redevelop individualistic ethical norms to match a network logic of power and responsibility.

Keywords Big Data • Ethics • Corporate moral agency • Network ethics • Network theory • Legal frameworks • Social network services • Moral network agency

INTRODUCTION

In May 2010, the website PatientsLikeMe.com, which provides a platform for people to share their worries about their diseases and exchange treatment protocols and medications, revealed a major intrusion. The Nielsen

A. Zwitter (✉)
Department of Political Science, University of Groningen, The Netherlands, UK

© The Editor(s) (if applicable) and The Author(s) 2016
A. Bunnik et al. (eds.), *Big Data Challenges*,
DOI 10.1057/978-1-349-94885-7_3

company, through its subsidiary BuzzMetrics, scraped all data from the forum, including otherwise secret medical information. Nielsen subsequently admitted that they were mining data from 130 million blogs, 8000 message boards, and several social media sites to sell it to advertisers, marketers, and pharmaceutical companies (Goodman 2015, chap. 4). Add that to the capabilities of actors like Anonymous and of national security agencies, and it becomes increasingly clear that traditional power distributions of a realist tradition and assumptions about the importance of individual agency are outdated when it comes to the cyber domain and the effects of Big Data. Individual agency, in these cases, seems to be pushed into the background, but so is the agency of the state. At the same time, non-state actors on the Big Data collection and utilisation side determine more and more the rules of international affairs in the cyber domain.

Big Data is generated in manifold ways: smart sensors, sky surveys, cell phone data, likes on Facebook, and so on. Big Data generated by individuals happens most of the time involuntarily and without their awareness. Yes, many know that the search queries they enter into Google, the geo-location movement patterns of our cell phones, or the comments on a friend's picture create a digital footprint. However, often we remain unaware of the aggressiveness and rigour of how this data is scraped by data miners, collected by data warehouses, and sold to data brokers. This essay will argue that specifically personal data, purposely collected by service providers and actors in the security sector (data harvesting), tends to soften our individual moral agency. The usage of Big Data, in contrast to classical statistical data, reveals much about individuals in the data pool in longitudinal form. Big Data researchers, also in the private domain, suddenly have access to sensitive information through the mining of social media, web-based data, and so on, the collection of which would, prior to the Big Data age, have been prohibited by any ethics committee. This problem of privacy is even more exacerbated as corporate agents, through the use of behavioural algorithms, learn much about the individual and are not driven by ethical consideration but by the desire for profit. The increasing network nature of Big Data and of our societal co-existence changes, however, fundaments of ethical theory.

The nature of Big Data and the means of analysis (for example, network analysis of metadata) raise their own specific ethical problems that nowadays go beyond the privacy consideration of the individual and ask questions about the privacy of communities against the collecting and tracking of group and network data, the security from manipulation, and education for appropriate internet use. Particularly concerned with the network nature of data, this paper argues that we might need to redevelop individualistic ethical norms to match a network logic of power and responsibility.

NOTIONS OF INDIVIDUAL AND CORPORATE MORAL AGENCY[1]

First of all, we have to contrast the assumptions of traditional ethical theories with the new assumptions introduced by Big Data. This section will sketch in brief how philosophers traditionally elaborated the separate conditions of moral agency. Furthermore, it will outline reasons why we needed to develop corporate moral agency.

The degree to which an entity possesses moral agency determines the responsibility of the entity. Moral responsibility in combination with extraneous and intrinsic factors, which escape the will (*volens*) of the entity, defines the culpability of this entity. In general, moral agency is determined through several entity-innate conditions three of which are commonly agreed upon (Noorman 2012):

1. There should be a causal connection between the person and the outcome of actions. A person is usually held responsible only if she had some control over the outcome of events.
2. The subject has to have knowledge of and be able to consider the possible consequences of her actions. We tend to excuse someone from blame if he or she could not have known that actions would lead to a harmful event.
3. The subject has to be able to freely choose to act in certain way. That is, it does not make sense to hold someone responsible for a harmful event if her actions were completely determined by outside forces.

Usually, moral agency is attributed to the individual human being. There are, however, ethical approaches that traditionally (implicitly or explicitly) assume moral agency also to be applicable to corporate entities, that is, entities that consist of more human beings, such as international relations (IR), international law, and just war theories.

Corporate moral agency is comparable to the legal fiction of corporate personhood. Morality and law in this instance are related: in order to make corporate entities culpable for morally impermissible actions or omissions, one needs to construct an agency that can bear moral responsibility. Let me first elaborate why individual and corporate (or institutional) moral agency is important in normative and empirical research on Ethics. Several reasons speak for the existence of corporate moral agency:

1. If only individuals are moral agents, one cannot attribute culpability and accountability to institutional (corporate) actors (Erskine 2010).
2. If collectivities have no agency, assigning duties to them and not to their individual constituent parts is meaningless (Erskine 2001).
3. Corporate moral agency is necessary to justify actions and responses of corporate agents. If only individuals are moral agents, one cannot attribute responsibility to institutional (corporate) actors such as states or the UN (Erskine 2001).
4. Corporate moral agency is necessary to justify individual duties derived from claims of the collective (for example, the collective right to claim taxes from the individual).
5. Corporate moral agency is necessary to justify individual culpability for enabling the wrongdoing of the corporate agency (cf. the criminal legal concept of joint criminal enterprise), in order to establish, for example, moral and legal responsibility of a member of a terrorist organisation who facilitates the action of the organisation by acts that *per se* are not unmoral, such as raising funds or providing social support for the public.

Even if, in philosophical terms, it might be difficult to ground and defend institutional moral agency (for example, due a corporate actor's incapability to feel pain and punishment and due to a lack of capability to empathy), these pragmatic reasons show why one also needs to think in terms of institutional moral agency.

Pragmatism has another effect: since actors in international relations behave as though states in particular, but increasingly also non-state corporate actors, have moral agency, this belief creates in essence behaviour that can only be explained if one incorporates such a constructed corporate moral agency into one's ontology. This reasoning can be said to be the normative force of the factual and it manifests itself not only in how actors behave in international affairs, but also in how researchers observe the world and how they think about it. Furthermore, people do identify with institutional agencies and feel harmed if their institution is being attacked or feel responsible for the wrongdoing of it (this, of course, depends on the strength of the emotional bond, and more research in this regard is necessary, particularly about national and religions sentiments). One of the preconditions of moral agency is the ability to act, or, in other words, to influence others. Collective intentionality is generally considered to be a problem (Lewis 1948; Downie 1969). However, Hobbes (2001) argues for such an agency when stating:

> A multitude of men are made "one" person when they are by one man or one person represented, so that it be done with the consent of every one of that multitude in particular. For it is the "unity" of the representer, not the "unity" of the represented, that maketh the person "one." And it is the representer that beareth the person, and but one person; and "unity" cannot otherwise be understood in multitude.

The ability to act in unity is traditionally given in the form of the state. Nowadays, however, non-state corporate actors dominate more and more the global moral domain. Their nature is very market-driven; that is, the individual in the lower hierarchy of the corporate agent is not represented but is employed and *nolens/volens* contributes to the action of the corporate agent. In other words, in the corporate agent of the non-state economic corporation we find the reversal of the social contract.

NETWORK ETHICS: TRANSCENDING AGENCY ALTOGETHER

We have seen that the individual in the service of the corporate agency is stripped of his or her agency when it comes to the actions of the corporate agency. Furthermore, network theory has fundamentally challenged the concept of the capability of the individual (a basic aspect of moral agency) on an ontological level by redefining the power of an agent as the entirety of its relations to other agents rather than its resources to act. If, in order to understand the effect of Big Data on our hyper-networked society, this logic is transferred to moral theory, we have to rethink the concept of individual and state agency.

First, the nature of the internet and the modus operandi employed by the actors inhabiting the cyber domain is dissolving traditional notions of the nation state and of national legislation. This dissolving became quite clear before the term Big Data became popular. Big Data, however, adds to this that practices such as data mining are inherently global in reach, and that the location of companies and data warehouses is strategically placed to circumvent national legislations that might limit these practices. A look at the Global Data Protection handbook reveals how many states do not have adequate data protection laws or any such laws at all.[2]

Second, the legal frameworks pioneered in the enlightenment period and still the legal standard of today, like human rights, are inherently designed around the individual actor and his or her specific individualistic interests, such as privacy. Big Data, however, is not so much about the individual but rather about the many, leaving the group vulnerable even if its individual members' privacy might by protected by their civil and political rights. Groups like consumers, ethnicities, cultures, football fans, and political parties all have their characteristics. In-depth analysis on the basis of ano-nymised data about their behaviour, their preferences, their dislikes, and so on might reveal vulnerabilities to be exploited for the purpose of social engineering and manipulation. Furthermore, such data might be used for political purposes to influence public opinion with half-facts; imagine populist right-wing parties requesting statistics of how much more likely it is that migrants commit a certain crime in comparison to non-migrants. This information might be used to politically support a stricter enforcement of migration policies, ignoring other underlying structural reasons for the results that might be just as applicable to other segments of society.

Third, the general public does not understand the phenomenon of Big Data well enough to be particularly concerned by it. Of course, whistle-blowers and investigative journalists once in a while are able to give glimpses into the reality of the cyber domain. But their efforts remain insufficient to create a general public awareness of the actual digital foot-print our internet presence and cell phones create. It remains unclear to the public that the use of this digital footprint, with concern for issues such as group privacy and manipulation of the masses, has already dwarfed individual privacy issues. Even if the 'right to be forgotten' makes sense in certain cases, applying it as an individual to one company at a time still leaves the hundreds of other actors that are also collecting the same data and which we do not know about entirely unaffected.

All these developments have pushed both individual agency and the agency of the state towards the background in favour of the corporate agency of technology companies, cyber activists and cyber caliphates, organised online crime, and so on.

In the Web of Big Data

This section explains how Big Data puts us as individuals into a web of interactions best explained ethically with network theory.

As elaborated in the previous chapter, the nature of Big Data is messy and organic. It is, however, not random. The organic structure of the data is much influenced by the information gathered through social network services (SNS), which interlink and cross-reference the individual data producer with others, exemplified by the friends' networks on Facebook, Linked-In connections, followers on Twitter, and so on. These interconnections represent a set of metadata that contains relational information, which, in conjunction with content-related information (such as posts about actions, geographic information, and pictures), gives a bird's eye picture of the behaviour of a person as visible in the person's digital footprint and real-world references the person makes and others make about the person. In other words, the individuals' actions (visible) on the web have implications not only for the person himself or herself, but for other persons that are digitally connected with this individual. Another feature is that the connections among persons stripped from contextual information can lead to misbalanced conclusions, which become ethically problematic, as, for example, in the following hypothetical case:

> Person A is active on SNS and digitally connected with B, C, and D. B and C are very good friends of A; D is a friend of C; D does not know B and has only met A once, after which A added D to his SNS contacts. A conducts a robbery.
>
> Independently from contextual information, we can only say that, based on the frequency of digital interactions, B and C are potential suspects regarding knowledge of the crime or complicity. D might know something.
>
> Only when adding the contextual layer do we find that A was in search of quick profit. A told B. B connected A with D, and D would tell A about the best way to conduct the robbery for a share of the bait. C was totally unaware of anything, but, according to SNA, the more likely suspect regarding knowledge or complicity.

This example aims to illustrate that data created within the Big Data sphere of SNS can be highly misleading when stripped of contextual information. If law enforcement agencies are basing their actions on social network data, the consequences for C could be entirely disproportionate to his moral culpability.

This leads to four intermediate conclusions, namely that:

1. It is irresponsible to make decisions in such a way.
2. Since we know that decisions can be made on circumstantial evidence, we are hurting others unintentionally by doing something that is not related to them but by the mere fact of SNS data.

3. There is a higher moral responsibility for those with many network connections and degree centrality.
4. Big Data collectors bear a uniquely specific burden of moral responsibility regarding decision-making based on the data they collect.

In summary, the individual is ethically responsible not only for its individual acts but for the entirety of his connections. Thus, ethical judgement is less about judging one act, but affects the entirety of a person's connections.

POWER IN NETWORK THEORY

According to Castells (2011), there are four forms of power in the network society:

1. Networking power: power exercised by networked actors over un-networked actors (power of exclusion).
2. Network power: power exercised over members of a network through imposing rules (power of inclusion).
3. Networked power: power of agenda-setting and managerial and editorial decision-making in the organisation of a network.
4. Network-making power: the power to establish and disable networks of communications.

Particularly with regard to (3), power is inherently relational (Hanneman and Riddle 2005). A's power is the degree to which B is dependent on A or, alternatively, A can influence B. That means that A's power is different vis-à-vis C. The more connections A has, the more power he can exert. This is referred to micro-level power and is understood as the concept of centrality (Bonacich 1987).[3] On the macro level, the whole network of A-B-C-D is dependent on the density of more or less inherent power.

These different perspectives on power give us an entirely different view of agency, namely an agency that is, for its capability of morally relevant action, entirely dependent on other actors. These other actors might be only passive recipients of harm; that is, they experience collateral damage. The network nature of society, however, means that this passive agency is always a factor when judging the moral responsibility of the active agent, that is, the one that commits or omits the morally relevant action.

CONSEQUENCES FOR MORAL NETWORK AGENCY

Shannon Vallor (2010) has already highlighted that virtue ethics might be an underutilised but very valuable approach to understanding social networking technologies and ethics. Vallor points out that a virtue-based perspective on information technology is needed to correct for a strong utilitarian bias in contemporary research methodologies. Very much in line with Vallor's idea, I argue that the nature of ethical ontology and phenomenology might be fundamentally changing through integrating the effect of the above-explained phenomena into a theory of network ethics:

1. Moral responsibility of corporate agency.
2. Reversal of the social contract.
3. Network character of power.
4. Network effect of moral actions, previously considered isolated.

These four phenomena suggest that the trend towards a hyper-networked society is increasing; the trend in tracking and linking SNS Big Data production and other personalised data is increasing; and the strengthening of corporate agency, in which individual moral agency is gradually reduced, makes ethical judgements more structure-dependent. These processes have epistemological consequences on what questions we can and have to ask in order to evaluate the moral content of actions.

If the unintentional network effect of moral action becomes increasingly severe, moral action will have to be increasingly judged on the basis of the collateral moral effect on passive agents. This means that, if one would want to assess the potential moral responsibility, social network analysis might become a tool for investigating the field of ethics. Such a view on networks and ethics would attribute a higher degree of moral responsibility to agents that are more densely embedded in social networks than others. In more technical terms, the different centralities (degree, betweeness, and closeness—that is, the network-theory-specific idea about power) define the extent to which an actor is culpable and the degree to which the actor actually possesses moral agency. If empirically substantiated, this theory has consequences for expectations of corporate actors, who have a higher degree of moral agency. Traditionally, the saying goes that 'with power comes responsibility'. That this can actually be measured with the tools of SNA has not been explored until now.

The choices to connect with others, for the most part, are independent of a specific morally relevant act. However, as the morally relevant act affects all connections made earlier in life through collateral network effects, one might consider looking more closely at the overall actions of a person or a corporate agency to judge the overall moral character. This, it seems, opens a different door to character-focused virtue ethics approaches in addition to Vallor's perspective.

CONCLUDING REMARKS ON BIG DATA IMPLICATIONS

This chapter pointed out that changing views towards a hyper-networked society and the collection of all digital footprints of actions through Big Data gathering has fundamental effects on contemporary ethical ontology. The networked collateral damage and the network-theory-informed idea of power lead to the conclusion that we might have to adapt our concept of ethical responsibility. The individual's ethical culpability is changing due to the mere collateral effect of every digital social connection, providing information about the individual and to the individual about his or her social connection. This inference leads to the conclusion that a character-focused virtue-ethics approach, which looks at the network affected through the behaviour of the individual agent, might become more and more indispensable to an understanding of moral responsibility.

Typically, corporate actors (corporations and states) have the ability to collect and utilise Big Data generated through SNS and other digital footprints of the individual. This gives corporate actors an unprecedented degree of power through information. At the same time, the state reaches its limits with regulating the cyber domain as soon as online transmissions cross borders. Attempts at international regulation, such as the EU-US Safe Harbour Framework, are plagued with ineffectiveness resulting, in part, from the corporate actors' attempts to circumvent issues of privacy and data protection. Another element of corporate power is the unique centrality that corporate agencies have due to being connected to an immense number of other agents (nodes). Finally, SNS controlling agents have a unique source of power through managing the rules of participation in, access to, and exclusion from networks, and through the ability to simply shut down networks. This power creates a moral responsibility that can only be compared to the responsibility of wielding power over weapons of mass effect. Finally, these considerations suggested that network theory and the tools of network analysis might become indispensable parts of contemporary ethical theory.

In conclusion, one can observe the effect that Big Data, and social media in particular, have on ontological assumptions about agency. What exactly this change will mean remains to be seen. Technology and the way we are using it are rapidly changing. Therefore, it is important to keep updating ethical theory to remain applicable to the new realities created by information technology.

NOTES

1. This section is based on Zwitter (2013).
2. Global Data Protection Handbook. Retrieved April 16, 2015, from http://dlapiperdataprotection.com/#handbook/world-map-section/c1_AR/c2_EG
3. Centrality is furthermore differentiated in degree-, closeness-, and between-ness centrality.

REFERENCES

Bonacich, P. (1987). Power and centrality: A family of measures. *American Journal of Sociology, 92*(5), 1170–1182.

Castells, M. (2011). A network theory of power. *International Journal of Communication, 5*, 773–787.

Downie, R. S. (1969). Collective responsibility. *Philosophy, 44*, 66–69.

Erskine, T. (2001). Assigning responsibilities to institutional moral agents: The case of states and quasi-states. *Ethics & International Affairs, 15*(2), 67–85.

Erskine, T. (2010). Kicking bodies and damning souls: The danger of harming 'innocent' individuals while punishing 'delinquent' states. *Ethics & International Affairs, 24*(3), 261–285.

Goodman, M. (2015). *Future crimes: Everything is connected, everyone is vulnerable and what we can do about it.* New York: Knopf Doubleday Publishing Group, Ebook.

Hanneman, R. A., & Riddle, M. (2005). *Introduction to social network methods.* Riverside, CA: University of California. Retrieved August 29, 2013, from http://faculty.ucr.edu/~hanneman/nettext/C10_Centrality.html

Hobbes, T. (2001). *The Harvard classics* (Of man, being the first part of Leviathan, Vol. 34, Pt. 5). New York: P.F. Collier & Son.

Lewis, H. D. (1948). Collective responsibility. *Philosophy, 24*, 3–18.

Noorman, M., (2012). Computing and moral responsibility. In E. N. Zalta (Ed.), *The stanford encyclopedia of philosophy* (Fall ed.). Retrieved from http://plato. stanford.edu/archives/fall2012/entries/computing-responsibility

Vallor, S. (2010). Social networking technology and the virtues. *Ethics and Information Technology, 12*(2), 157–170.

Zwitter, A. (2013). Ethical research in law and politics: Methodological pitfalls. In H. Bashir, P. Gray, & E. Masad (Eds.), *Co-existing in a globalized world* (pp. 47–62). Plymouth: Lexington Books.

CHAPTER 4

Security Networks and Human Autonomy: A Philosophical Investigation

David Lundie

Abstract Data transactions in complex information networks have their own philosophical and mathematical logics. This chapter introduces the reader to key philosophical debates about the nature and effect of information technologies, and seeks to apply these to the philosophy of information. Drawing on personalist philosophy, the chapter redirects attention to questions of moral agency as they relate to security and intelligence work, and questions whether overreliance on data may fail to account for important aspects of human experience and action.

Keywords Security networks • Human autonomy • Philosophy of information • Information technologies • Surveillance • Dividuation • Personalistic philosophy • Values in design

INTRODUCTION

This chapter highlights and critically examines the philosophical assumptions which have governed the developments of online networks in the early stages of their evolution. These assumptions, drawn from the philosophy of mathematics, carry with them their own definitions of knowledge, intelligence, and security, which are not always compatible with the working

D. Lundie (✉)
Department of Education Studies, Liverpool Hope University, Liverpool, UK

© The Editor(s) (if applicable) and The Author(s) 2016   35
A. Bunnik et al. (eds.), *Big Data Challenges*,
DOI 10.1057/978-1-349-94885-7_4

definitions either in the intelligence community or in the wider human domain. Drawing on a few practical examples, this chapter examines some of the critical incidents which can result from this mismatch of design and purpose, and proposes an approach to values in design which can mitigate these concerns. The legal traditions of the Western world have always recognised the importance of *mens rea*—intent or culpability—to criminality or threat response, and this distinction stands in contrast to many unstructured approaches to Big Data analytics, which rely only on correlations and probabilities. This issue raises real ethical problems for intelligence and security—for example, whether to place someone on a watch list because he or she shares a pattern of online buying with known terrorists, or take pre-emptive action against protestors whose activities have been 'shared' and publicised, perhaps without their knowledge, by extremists on social networking sites.

From its beginnings, information technology has engaged questions about the nature of information, and how to ensure its effective transmission and correspondence with the world. Initially, these questions were largely concerned with the authentication of truth values in the communication of information—how could one remote server be sure of having received the message correctly and be sure of the identity of the sender? Such seemingly simple questions rest on a complex theory of knowledge, requiring functional definitions of intelligence (Turing 1949) and knowledge (Shannon and Weaver 1949). These questions lend themselves more easily to mathematical analysis than to philosophical ethics. For many years, information ethics remained largely confined to the design of efficient systems with effective fail-safe devices—in designing a system for aircraft to communicate with air traffic control, an authentication failure could lead to a crash and loss of life. According to this version of information ethics, a system is 'good' in the moral sense when it is 'good' in the sense of efficient, whilst the design or use of the system is 'inherently value neutral' (Alder 1998). An increasing number of voices in a range of fields have recently drawn attention, however, to the ethical issues which reside in the design process itself (Knobel and Bowker 2011; Wicker and Schrader 2010). Arguably, systems may pose ethical problems by being too efficient (Cohen 2000) and by changing social interactions amongst human operators in detrimental ways, either by design or accidental (Friedman and Nissenbaum 1996).

There is a dawning recognition that technology has the potential not only to increase the efficiency of intelligence work, but to change the nature and meaning of our understandings of intelligence. From the expanding portfolios of traditional intelligence and security organisations such as Parsons and Lockheed Martin into training and consultancy for banks, retail chains, and public transportation to the estimated 68,000 closed-circuit television (CCTV) cameras in English secondary schools, the scale and definition of intelligence work are redefined by ubiquitous surveillance technologies. It is not only the scale and availability of equipment, however, that change the landscape, but the nature of human–computer interaction itself, and the information archive that this interaction creates.

DIVIDUATION, SURVEILLANCE, AND THE PERSON

In his brief but seminal *Postscript on the Societies of Control*, Gilles Deleuze highlights what he sees as a fundamental shift in the locus of control in information societies. Whereas the earlier *disciplinary* societies functioned by enclosing people in spaces, schools, factories, army barracks, or prisons, Deleuze argues that the information society exerts its control in a new way, by *dividuation* (1992). Whilst many of the most vocal critics of the digital society have pointed to a 'digital panopticon', evoking Bentham's prison *par excellence*, Deleuze argues that digital society divides the individual amongst ceaseless entailments which make a claim on his identity:

> The family, the school, the army, the factory are no longer the distinct analogical spaces that converge towards an owner—state or private power—but coded figures—deformable and transformable—of a single corporation that now has only stockholders. (1992, p. 6)

The work e-mail at 6 a.m., the educational podcast to listen to at the gym, and the surveillance of map searches triangulated against road tolls all point to the dividuation of the subject, according to Deleuze's theory.

Whilst, on the surface, this analysis appears to be concerned with the neoliberal politics of the corporation, this chapter focuses on a more troubling informational ontology on which these dividual identities rest. The information ontology which underpins much of the world of Big Data offers an illusion of totalising control, but is, I argue, fundamentally flawed as an ontology of human agency, reducing knowledge to information and intelligence to algorithms. The origins of this information ontology and its consequences for politics and society have so far been of little concern in either political or academic discussions on security. This chapter, and the wider book, is one contribution towards exposing it to sustained critique.

Ever since Plato first questioned the written word supplanting the art of dialogue (*Phaedrus* 276e–277a), philosophers have been raising concerns about the social effects of technology. For Heidegger, *techné* denotes a form of knowledge or experience of being: the artist, craftsman, or technician causes beings to come forth, be revealed, and become present to the technician as knower (Heidegger 1978, p. 184). In this becoming present, Heidegger argues, something is known; there is an informational content to the technology as a mediator. In the language of information science, this informational content can be called 'operational data', which relate to the operation, use, and performance of the system itself (Floridi 2004, p. 43). In a search for clarity, we must acknowledge this concern and this difference—one can imagine the first ancient spy to report to his king that he had seen the plans written on parchment but had not looked into the opponent's *eyes* to know if he was lying. Moving beyond this ages-old humint/sigint dichotomy involves recognising that any technology generates information about its own usage, data which adds a *hypertext*, or a text-about-a-text, to the information it seeks to communicate.[1]

The technologies which support the Big Data industry have the additional properties of being digital, interactive, and data-acquisitive. They collect and process data by assigning it numerical (specifically binary) variables (the responses to yes/no questions). Some theorists have regarded such binaries as being not only the foundation of all knowledge (true/false binaries), but also the foundation of the physical world (is/is-not binaries) (Wheeler 1990). Regardless of the answer we might give to such philosophical speculation, the conceptualisation of the world in digital binary terms raises important questions for decision-making in the human sphere, as this chapter will illustrate. Furthermore, these technologies are interactive—they are intended to facilitate communication between two or more intelligent agents. To be successful at this task, the interaction of each agent with the mediating technology must also be successful (Ess 2009). Finally, these technologies are data-acquisitive—their effectiveness at carrying out their function depends on the acquisition and distribution of information. In some cases, this data acquisition has a clear and obvious connection to the function of the system (for example, a CCTV camera designed to detect and deter criminal activity). In other cases, however, this acquisition has a less obvious, and, at times, unnecessary, role in the design of the system (Wicker and Schrader 2010). For example, kinaesthetic game controllers for games consoles collect extensive and fine-grained data on individual players' gait and range of motion. Whilst this information can be used to improve the gameplay experience, it is also of value in identifying individual players in ways that would not be detectable otherwise. Further ethical questions arise when data acquired in one context (such as the game controller) is combined with data from another context (such as the CCTV camera) to enable the observer to identify an individual image by his gait or running style—these may be described as problems of contextual integrity or information dissemination (Van den Hoven 1997; Solove 2006). To illustrate some of these complexities, the digital ethicist David Riphagen uses the example of an embarrassing photo taken at a party:

First, the photo is taken at the party (Solove's information collection), and not many people would judge this as immoral. The picture is posted online (Solove's information processing), and as long as this would happen on a website that allows restricted access in addition to the subject's consent, this also is not very objectionable. The problems start when the photo is disseminated (Solove's information dissemination) to people without the subject's consent. The picture might be disclosed to persons belonging to a social sphere within which the subject does not want the photo to be disclosed (Van den Hoven's informational injustice). Furthermore, by tagging the photo with the subject's real name, the photo can become the basis for scrutiny by future employers (Van den Hoven's information-based harm). Because the users cannot unbundle the services from the [social network], he cannot ex ante prevent the dissemination from happening (Van den Hoven's informational inequality). Finally, if the photo is disclosed to people that the subject does not know, he does not have the freedom to present his moral identity to the people as he wants, as those people already have an image of him (Van den Hoven's restriction on moral autonomy and pre-emption of moral identity). (Riphagen 2008, p. 29)

This gives a glimpse into the plurality of moral questions raised by Big Data. The growing interest in, and capacity for, the systematic acquisition and mining of fine-grained demographic data and its applications in improving business performance are of interest to security in a range of contexts. The same algorithm development process designed to target advertising or predict corporate behaviour has applications for the state, for corporate intelligence, and for other non-state actors in the security space. Big Data and its attendant tangle of technological, socio-legal, economic, and moral questions have become a growing area of interest, not only in academic literature, but also in media, policy, and public debate.

The technologies employed in this large-scale acquisition of digital data are not value-neutral, and rely on assumptions of what counts as meaningful, the origins of which are to be found in an information-theoretic account of knowledge which is problematic for traditional conceptualisations of 'intelligence'.

INFORMATION THEORY AND THE MEANING
AND DEFINITION OF DATA

The information-theoretic account of knowledge attempts to address a problem of linking truth, knowledge, and justification without including any factor besides information. The account may be defined, formally, as:

> K knows that s is F = K's belief that s is F is caused (or causally sustained) by the information that s is F. (Adams 2004)

I read in *The New York Times* that Google has changed its privacy policy, and this information causes me to believe that Google has indeed changed its policy. That information comes from a chain of causes by which the author came to know the facts about Google's policy change. The information that *The New York Times* is not used to printing erroneous stories, or that it is not April 1st, may be part of my account of coming to believe this story, but this is not some other form of justification. It is merely 'metadata', information about information. On this account, there is nothing in the causal chain that justifies my knowledge besides information. Such an account is highly satisfactory when designing systems for information authentication and transmission, and consequently occupies a prominent place amongst philosophers of computing. Using it to define all human-knowledge-justifying processes, however, is much more problematic.

Whilst constructing an account of knowledge that rests entirely on information appears to solve a number of philosophical problems, the information-theoretic account has a number of problems. First, by positing no justification for knowledge other than information, this account simply shifts questions of truth away from knowledge and onto data. Second, although we may begin with a definition of information that is watertight about the truthfulness of 'x is information that p if [and only if] p [is true]' (Dretske 1981), the realities of information systems are such that the information flow contains both true and false data, information and misinformation, data and noise. The larger and messier the datasets we rely on, the harder it becomes to separate the two.

A promising response to this problem draws on the mathematical theory of communication (Shannon and Weaver 1949); the amount of information needed to justify knowledge of x is inversely proportional to the probability of x. I have left my front door locked or unlocked. There are two possible states, so one piece of information can tell me whether it is locked or not. The information that there is one unlocked door on my street, however, requires many more variables to narrow it down to the correct door. The less likely a state of affairs, the greater the quantity of information required to reduce its probability to 100%.

Whilst this account is associated with the philosophy of computing and information, its origins run much deeper into the early days of industrialisation. Then, as now, new technological innovations led philosophers to question traditional theories and explanatory accounts of human behaviour. Then, as now, the physical world appeared to offer a perfectly sufficient causal account of being without the need for an appeal to immateriality. In 1749, Julien Offray de La Mettrie posited that the human brain held no immaterial element, no ghost was required in the machine, and the human machine could be explained without recourse to values or ends, simply in terms of chains of 'secondary' causes. What La Mettrie described in terms of the physical machine, Dretske (1981) posits in terms of information processing, making him perhaps the first to articulate the information-theoretic account of knowledge. '[S]ounds or words, which are transmitted from one person's mouth, through another's ear and into his brain' (de La Mettrie 1996, p. 13)—the stark formulation of the Enlightenment *philosophe* captures the causal account: knowledge rests on information transmission as cause, not as communication or justification. My reading an article concerned about Google's privacy policy, on this account, is substantially the same as seeing its consequences; all justification, from the senses, from my reflections, from media, or from the intimate communication of a friend, is information and information alone. In speculating about the ability to teach sign language to apes, La Mettrie also acts as precursor to another staple of the philosophy of information: the natural-language-use test for artificial intelligence (Turing 1949). If an animal, or a machine, can use information and can act as a link in the causal chain in a way indistinguishable from a human, it is, on this account, intelligent.

A fundamental problem with this account can be observed when it comes to human beings, however. Whereas the information-theoretic account assumes that there is a causal channel that can exist between an information sender and an information recipient, it is not at all clear that this is the case when it comes to conscious subjects. Digital information systems use essentially the same structures of language to process data internally as they do to transmit and verify that data, whereas human consciousness does not admit of a truly private language. Without shared systems of meaning, the conscious subject is unable to give meaning to the data of immediate experience (Wittgenstein 1953). As such, information-theoretic ways of thinking about knowledge are unable to account for what may be termed 'ipseity' or 'myness', the unnoticed awareness of a self as the subject of our experiences of knowing (Zahavi and Parnas 1998; Lundie 2016). I am not only self-aware when I am reflecting on the fact that it is *me* who is sitting at my desk, and not another, but also, on a much more basic level, pre-reflectively aware of my feelings of boredom or interest. The myness of these experiences is not an additional item of meta-data—information about the general experience of boredom to which the attribute 'mine' can be added—but my perception is an experience which requires no causal channel to make manifest its myness (Zahavi 2005). The value of information for calculating probabilities and the value of myness to a human-perceiving subject are not the same thing, nor can one be exchanged for the other.

The implications of data analytics for intelligence work, as for all forms of symbolic analysis which traditionally characterise many professional occupations (Reich 1992), are far-reaching. Because data analytics 'operate... at the traditionally human level of control in enabling the achievement of any and all objectives, *we cannot expect to discover or design new requirements for control that only people can fulfil*' (Spencer 1996, p. 73). The formerly human element of controlling processes of theorisation; approaches to the organisation and deployment of information, now alienated; and control of the means of surveillance are no longer solely the preserve of the human. Intelligence in the societies of control goes beyond the system of checks and balances of the traditional hierarchical organisation. Transmission and production of information are coterminous; quality control and production are one process. For the programmable information processor, nothing is gained by work which is not already inherent in its programmed nature; cause is no longer separable from effect. What can this kind of real-term, theory-free, agent-free process look like? And should we accept it as an authentic form of intelligence?

AGENCY, AUTONOMY, AND INFORMATION

Whilst a book on intelligence and Big Data may not seem like an appropriate venue for speculations on the existence of the soul, what is clear is that, for the first time in history, questions of the exceptional quality of human consciousness are no longer abstract and theoretical. Although La Mettrie's quarrel with Descartes was purely abstract, individuality is still being underdetermined at the level that "the most subtle anatomical study cannot discover" (de La Mettrie 1996, p. 10). Today, the increasing ability to determine outcome and the decreasing distance between cause and effect create the very real possibility of reducing human autonomy to 'the simple stimulus-response behaviour sought by direct marketers' (Cohen 2000, p. 1400). Without the need to posit an immaterial ego-soul, as Descartes did, we can, nonetheless, argue for something constitutive of human agency which is both distinct from this stimulus-response and independent of chains of informational causes. That distinction is manifested in materially significant ways, not merely as a reflective soul but as a being in the social, political, and informational world.

Some commentators have sought to counter this threat by positing a right to underdetermined environment, a space free from this kind of data micromanagement, in which human subjects can develop an authentic autonomy. Such attempts remain fated to failure on a number of grounds, however, in that they require a regulatory framework that is, by its nature, restricted to territorial sovereignty and unable to keep pace with technological developments (Tse et al. 2015). More pertinent, however, these approaches accept the information-theoretic account of knowledge. Human beings, on this account, really are at risk of being nothing more than processors, and need some enclosure in which to preserve their distinctiveness to avoid the inevitable consequences that follow from this conclusion. Not only is this approach insufficient, but it is unnecessary to the cultivation of the human subject, as human ipseity or human myness is irreducible to the information stream.

The information age has given rise to a new intelligence problem with implications for educators, theorists, analysts, and the economics of human capital: problems that are 'too big to know' (Weinberger 2012). By way of example, a team of researchers in physics and engineering from two research-intensive universities in the UK collaborated on the design of the cooling and vacuum system for the Vertex Locator of CERN's Large Hadron Collider. The complexity of such a system, in which the design of one sub-component exceeds the expertise of any one research lab, let alone any one human researcher, is illustrative of this problem. Our intuitive definitions of intelligence are challenged when faced with a technology, clearly brought forth by agency, yet about which no one individual can comprehensively lay claim to 'knowing' how it works. In these kinds of operations, it is not any one individual who is in charge of understanding the problem, but the network itself. It may also be the case in intelligence settings that the most dangerous part of a terrorist network may not be a named individual, but the network itself. In the construction of such complex systems, it is important for security services to be aware of the possible biases and informational harms which can be generated not only by miscommunicating data, but by communicating data accurately but outside of the context or level of analysis within which it has meaning. The data on the functioning of the cooling system at CERN must not be misinterpreted as the data from the collider itself.

A second and related problem involves the large quantities of metadata that can now be gathered about the ways in which people come to know. This shifts the emphasis of intelligence gathering from the content of human interactions to the means by which those interactions are mediated. Metadata is information according to the general definition, and it is meaningful when used to calculate the probability of a given state of affairs; how likely is it that Smith is a terrorist given his patterns of email correspondence? However, it is not information of the kind associated with myness, consciously willed dispositions, or committed assertions about a given state of affairs. It is for this reason that it is often related to deindividuation—the way in which users lose the ability to identify other stakeholders in their actions (Loch and Conger 1996, p. 76). Individuals generate data without having any conscious sense of doing so—the patterns of keystrokes as an individual types can be used to identify him or her, for example. This metadata can be aggregated across contexts to produce a comprehensive picture of an individual and has a remarkable predictive capacity, yet entirely ignores conscious human subjectivity.

A personalistic philosophy of mind, which suggests that something of the myness of human experience is not reducible to a causal chain (Lundie 2015), is borne out by empirical investigation (Schrader and Lundie 2012). Under experiment conditions, it is very difficult for people to attach stable value to their personal private information. Human agents are distinguished from robots, databases, and Turing machines not by their response to any given problem set (Floridi 2005), but because they value their own information incommensurably with information in the abstract.

My mother's maiden name has an exchange value as the password to my bank account, but it has another value for my memory, heritage, and family. This latter is an indexical value; it is mine not because ownership of it was transferred to me, but because its having value in this way is inseparable from and simultaneous with its being mine.

Conclusions

In summary, the challenges posed by Big Data for intelligence gathering in the societies of control require of us a conceptualisation of human agency and knowledge which is not reducible to either the control of means of information production or the accumulation of data on raw probabilities. As a function of the simultaneous production-transmission-analysis of data, data analytics may be in both senses an 'efficient cause'—serving as a second-order means to an end and as an increasingly effective link in a chain of information—and are ultimately insufficient to understand the indexical and agentive element of human activity. By recognising that algorithms used to analyse data are not value-neutral and, by initiating a conversation between intelligence professionals, human rights lawyers, and systems designers, it is possible to create an authentic technology of intelligence which both resists the temptation to panoptic accumulation of everything and enhances the human element in the system.

Intelligence professionals, like many others, find themselves working in collaboration across many fields more so than in the past, when 'secrets' were jealously guarded. Professionals from other fields, including information science, will bring with them their own competing perspectives on what constitutes meaningful information, and how it ought to be valued. Such approaches bring opportunities as well as threats. The threat that an over-determined informational environment can lead to an intelligence dystopia in which an overload of metadata elides human individuality and freedom, whilst also constraining analysis away from divergent thinking, may drive institutions in the opposite direction: to eschew data analytics. The opportunity to develop authentic systems of analysis, however, is too great to resist such technologies wholesale. By recognising the uniquely human element and the myness of human subjective experience and acknowledging that some forms of information are simply not reducible to easily predictive patterns, we can create systems that are both more innovative and more ethically sensitive.

Such an approach, however, requires new skills of technological, ethical, and inter-professional awareness from intelligence professionals;

it requires a new skill set of practical wisdom for the information age. How traditional intelligence agencies and their public paymasters respond to the potential for both good and ill posed by this new data ontology will be the crucial factor in creating ethically sensitive innovation and avoiding the frightening prospects of both a strangulated human autonomy and a hardened information culture.

NOTE

1. This sentence was written using MSWord and is being read on an e-Reader device.

REFERENCES

Adams, F. (2004). Knowledge. In Floridi, L. (ed.) The Blackwell Guide to the Philosophy of Computing and Information. Oxford: Blackwell. 228–236.

Alder, G. S. (1998). Ethical issues in electronic performance monitoring: A consideration of deontological and teleological perspectives. *Journal of Business Ethics, 17,* 729–743.

Cohen, J. (2000). Examined lives: Informational privacy and the subject as object. *Stanford Law Review, 53*(3), 1373–1438.

de La Mettrie, J. O. (1996). *Machine man and other writings.* Cambridge: Cambridge University Press.

Deleuze, G. (1992). Postscript on the societies of control. *October, 59,* 3–7.

Dretske, F. I. (1981). *Knowledge and the flow of information.* Cambridge, MA: MIT Press.

Ess, C. (2009). Floridi's philosophy of information and information ethics: Current perspectives, future directions. *Information Society, 25*(3), 159–168.

Floridi, L. (2004). Information. In L. Floridi (Ed.), *The Blackwell guide to the philosophy of computing and information.* Oxford: Blackwell.

Floridi, L. (2005). Consciousness, agents and the knowledge game. *Minds and Machines, 15*(3), 415–444.

Friedman, B., & Nissenbaum, H. (1996). Bias in computer systems. *ACM Transactions on Information Systems, 14*(3), 330–347.

Heidegger, M. (1978). *Basic writings: Revised and expanded edition.* London: Routledge.

Knobel, C., & Bowker, G. C. (2011). Computing ethics values in design. *Communications of the ACM, 54*(7), 26–28.

Loch, K. D., & Conger, S. (1996). Evaluating ethical decision making and computer use. *Communications of the ACM, 39,* 74–83.

Lundie, D. (2015). The givenness of the human learning experience and its incompatibility with information analytics. *Educational Philosophy and Theory.* doi:10.1080/00131857.2015.1052357.

Lundie, D. (2016). Authority, autonomy and automation: The irreducibility of pedagogy to information transactions. In *Studies in philosophy and education.* New York: Springer.

Plato (n.d.). Phaedrus. In *The works of Plato* (trans: Jowett, B.). New York: Tudor Publishing Co.

Reich, R. (1992). *The work of nations: Preparing ourselves for 21st century capitalism.* New York: Vintage.

Riphagen, D. (2008). The online panopticon: Privacy risks for users of social network sites. Retrieved November 27, 2015, from http://www.tbm.tudelft.nl/fileadmin/Faculteit/TBM/Over_de_Faculteit/Afdelingen/Afdeling_Infrastructure_Systems_and_Services/Sectie_Informatie_en_Communicatie_Technologie/medewerkers/jan_van_den_berg/news/doc/DavidRiphagen_GraduationThesis_Web.pdf

Schrader, D. & Lundie, D. (2012). *The value of privacy and private information sharing in online communications.* Association of Moral Education Annual Conference, San Antonio, TX, November 2012.

Shannon, C. E., & Weaver, W. (1949). *The mathematical theory of communication.* Urbana, IL: University of Illinois Press.

Solove, D. (2006). A taxonomy of privacy. *University of Pennsylvania Law Review, 154*(3), 477–559.

Spencer, G. (1996). Microcybernetics as the meta-technology of pure control. In Z. Sardar & J. R. Ravetz (Eds.), *Cyberfutures: Culture and politics on the information superhighway* (pp. 61–76). London: Pluto Press.

Tse, J., Schrader, D., Ghosh, D., Liao, T., & Lundie, D. (2015). A bibliometric analysis of privacy and ethics in IEEE Security and Privacy. *Ethics and Information Technology, 17*(2), 153–163.

Turing, A. (1949). Intelligent machinery, s.l., s.n.

Van den Hoven, M. J. (1997). Privacy and the varieties of moral wrong-doing in the information age. *Computers and Society, 27*(2), 33–37.

Weinberger, D. (2012). *Too big to know: Rethinking knowledge now that the facts aren't the facts, experts are everywhere, and the smartest person in the room is the room.* New York: Basic Books.

Wheeler, J. (1990). Information, physics, quantum: The search for links. In W. Zureck (Ed.), *Complexity, entropy and the physics of information.* Redwood City, CA: Addison Wesley.

Wicker, S. B., & Schrader, D. E. (2010). Privacy aware design principles for information networks. *Proceedings of the IEEE, 99*(2), 330–350.

Wittgenstein, L. (1953). *Philosophical investigations.* Oxford: Blackwell.

Zahavi, D. (2005). *Subjectivity and selfhood: Investigating the first-person perspective.* Cambridge, MA: MIT Press.

Zahavi, D., & Parnas, J. (1998). Phenomenal consciousness and self-awareness: A phenomenological critique of representational theory. *Journal of Consciousness Studies, 5*(5), 687–705.

CHAPTER 5

Is There a Press Release on That? The Challenges and Opportunities of Big Data for News Media

Anthony Cawley

Abstract This chapter reflects on the growing importance of data to journalism. It highlights the fact that data journalists are developing innovative forms of news storytelling which not only engage audiences in novel ways, but also offer greater transparency to the editorial production process. It argues, however, that data journalism finds itself caught in a long-standing tension in news industries between the dual demands on news to serve the public good (maintaining an informed citizenry and acting as a watchdog on power) and succeed as a for-profit informational commodity. The chapter suggests that, so far, data journalism aligns more comfortably with the public good objectives of news than with its commercial imperatives, which may be a factor limiting its wider practice in news organisations.

Keywords Data journalism • Data-driven news • Automated journalism • News industries • News narratives • Informational commodity • Public good • Watchdog role • Big Data • Security

A. Cawley (✉)
Department of Media and Communication, Liverpool Hope University, Liverpool, UK

© The Editor(s) (if applicable) and The Author(s) 2016   49
A. Bunnik et al. (eds.), *Big Data Challenges*,
DOI 10.1057/978-1-349-94885-7_5

INTRODUCTION

'A rapidly changing media landscape' is a phrase that has been used so often since the mainstream take-up of internet in the 1990s that it has become a cliché. But it continues to be rolled out by academics, industry executives, and practitioners because few, if any, aspects of the media are escaping significant digital transformation. Industry and organisational structures, business models, professional roles, and ways of engaging audiences have all been shaken out of their old certainties.

Change sketches a continuous line through the media's history, but the deep imprint of recent upheavals has been extraordinary. Destabilising matters further has been the global financial crisis, which, in bringing a harsher economic climate, has threatened the commercial health, and even survival, of many media organisations. In this broad context, the newsmedia, through data journalism, is grappling with the implications of Big Data for society in general and for the news industry in particular.

What the implications actually are is unclear. Neither is it certain that Big Data represents, in a journalistic sense, something new. But journalism's growing attachment to data connects to unresolved questions in the centuries-long development of news. What is the core purpose of news? What are the appropriate forms in which to tell a news story? What kinds of information should journalists seek as supporting evidence? And who has the authority to decide what is newsworthy?

At the heart of these questions is a historical uncertainty: should news be classed primarily as a public good or a product? Journalists tend to adopt a public good view of news, and they see its value in maintaining informed citizenries in democratic societies and in holding the powerful to account. Managers of media companies are more likely to position news as an informational commodity to be sold for profit (Cole and Harcup 2010). In the commercial settings in which most journalism is conducted, the two perspectives often grate against each other. News output that benefits the bottom line may not support quality journalism, and vice versa.

Even as a green shoot on the media landscape, data journalism blends naturally into the public good view of news: in pitching data through inventive forms of story-telling, journalists have opportunities to strengthen their relationships with audiences and sharpen their detection of state and corporate misconduct. However, data journalism faces significant obstacles, both internal and external to the news industry, if it is to deliver on that potential.

To provide a fuller context to data journalism's emergence, this chapter will consider the practice's historical roots alongside the findings of recent academic research. Then, in a brief case study, it will outline how data journalism is emerging in the Republic of Ireland. The country's media market sustains relatively small news organisations which operate under tighter financial, editorial, and technological resource constraints than leading-edge exponents of data journalism in bigger media markets such as the United Kingdom (UK) and the USA. The Irish case illustrates how the harnessing of Big Data to journalism is uneven both within national media markets and across the international sphere and is influenced significantly by non-technological factors, including legislative frameworks, news industry commercial pressures, journalistic cultures, and professional norms. The chapter will conclude with a discussion of the challenges confronting data journalism's continued development.

A Long Time Coming: Journalism Meets Big Data

One of the hopes being pinned to Big Data is that it will help journalists craft easy-to-understand accounts of what is happening in complex and fast-changing societies. That journalism is struggling to explain the world on which it reports is a long-standing anxiety. In the 1920s, the American public intellectual Walter Lippmann argued that the political-economic system had developed beyond the comprehension of the average citizen, whose life was being impacted by 'unnamed' or 'invisible powers' managed at 'distant centres' (Lippmann 2009: 3; first published in 1927). At this point, the news-media might be expected to step forward to ease the average citizen's confusion. But Lippmann claimed that 'no newspaper reports his environment so that he can grasp it' (2009, pp. 3–4). The problem for 1920s journalism was that the complexities of the political-economic system had slipped beyond its had slipped beyond its grasp, also.

When Lippmann was lamenting the limitations of print journalism almost ninety years ago, he was not, of course, referring to Big Data. Unwittingly, though, he was turning in that direction when he spotted the tendency of capitalistic societies to produce greater volumes of specialised information. In a decade in which the word 'media' itself was still a novelty (Briggs and Burke 2005), Lippmann believed journalism had already been overwhelmed by the scale and sophistication of capitalism's informational structures and was failing in its informed-citizenry and watchdog roles.

Capitalism's complexity would escalate through the twentieth century. In parallel, as the decades slipped by, news evolved to populate newer media forms: radio, television, and the internet. But this progress was not necessarily matched by an enhanced capacity to communicate the complexities of capitalistic societies as they attracted labels such as 'post-industrial society' or 'information society'. The global financial crisis that surfaced in the late 2000s illustrated the difficulties news media face in trying to report on advanced capitalism in a meaningful manner to the public. As the crisis deepened, even specialist business journalists were found to lack the skills, expertise, and resources properly to investigate, understand, and critique the intricate products and models emerging from the financial sector (Doyle 2006; Tambini 2010; Fahy 2014; O'Brien 2015).

Journalism's limited explanatory and critical capacities can be tied to news industry structures and commercial demands. Producing original journalistic content, especially from longer-term investigative projects, is time consuming, labour intensive, expensive, and risky (not all investigations will lead to a publishable story). News industry economics have evolved to favour cheaper, reliable, and predictable sources of information, including public relations material and regular journalistic 'beats' such as parliaments and courts. A contemporary of Lippmann's, the social commentator Upton Sinclair, recognised in the 1920s the eagerness of American newspapers to republish as news the information supplied by the government and the business sector (Sinclair 2003; first published in 1920). These actors were motivated to feed material to journalists to gain favourable publicity in the news, or, at a minimum, to dull criticism. Some sixty years later, Oscar Gandy (1982) called the practice an 'information subsidy', in the sense that governments, corporate actors, and public relations professionals were subsidising the cost of news production for commercial media organisations.

Lewis et al. (2008) argue that the news media's dependence on supplied material is likely to increase in the future. One reason is that newsroom resources are being hollowed out as news organisations try to carve out sustainable business models in the digital economy. Also, given that governmental and corporate actors tend to maintain efficient public relations units, the supply of pre-packaged 'news' is unlikely to run dry. Within this supply-demand relationship is, perhaps, a point of added interest to data journalists. The core activities of governmental and corporate actors increasingly rely on the gathering, processing, and manipulation of Big Data. To date, however, data sets have fallen outside the conventional provision to journalists of press releases, prepared statements, and verbal briefings.

ACADEMIC VIEWS OF JOURNALISM AND BIG DATA

The academic literature on data journalism remains 'relatively sparse' (Franklin 2014, p. 485). However, media scholars are directing greater attention to developments in the area as more journalists rely on 'data-processing tools' to highlight social issues and expose wrongdoing (Parasie 2015, p. 364). Specifically, media scholars are trying to gauge the disruptions and continuities between data journalism and traditional journalistic values, practices, and ethics. Attracting significant research interest is the potential of data journalism to break free of the news industry's obsession with immediacy and allow stories to unfold over longer periods of time (Anderson 2015).

From the public's perspective, the most visible impact of data journalism has been the increase in news stories told through infographics, interactive visualisations, and probability models (Lewis and Westlund 2015). In a move to increase editorial transparency, some data journalists have been making their data sets publicly available to facilitate audience engagement and analysis (Lewis and Westlund 2015). Their actions are a marked departure from conventional news production, which traditionally has been closed to outside scrutiny.

The recent turn to data signals a broadening of the kinds of information that journalists consider legitimate to underpin news stories. The shift has historical precedent. Newspapers used to publish stories gathered almost exclusively from information from documents (Anderson 2015). Only in the late nineteenth century did the interview emerge in Anglo-American and Irish journalism as a technique to gather first-hand information from people (Anderson 2015).

Evaluating data journalism through a historical lens reveals that the principles underlying it are decades old (Anderson 2015). Having surveyed infographics in 1940s American newspapers, Anderson concluded that 'data aggregation and information visualisation have been part of journalism for a long time' (2015, p. 351). In a similar vein, Parasie and Dagiral (2013) point out that the meshing of electronic data and journalism emerged, through computer-assisted reporting, in the 1960s. They suggest that, in its modern guise, data journalism could contribute to democracy in three key ways: through increased journalistic objectivity, the offering of new tools to keep a check on government actions, and increasing citizens' participation.

The roots of data journalism may be deeper than expected, but the practice still holds the potential to spark radical transformations in the news industry. For instance, Carlson highlights the emergence of 'automated journalism', where human reporters largely are displaced from news production and algorithms recast data sets as news narratives (2015, p. 416). He identifies as an example *The Washington Post*'s Truth Teller app, which runs real-time accuracy checks on politicians' speeches (http://truthteller.washingtonpost.com/). Such initiatives, Carlson suggests, are part of a wider 'movement of Big Data from newsgathering aid to the production of news itself' (2015, p. 417). For this reason, he argues, automated journalism calls into question traditional notions of news work and what constitutes journalistic authority if human editors and journalists are sidelined.

Lewis and Westlund caution that, amid all the 'hype' and 'hope' associated with Big Data, it is impossible to know what will happen, but it is becoming increasingly apparent that '*something* important is changing' (2015, p. 448). From the perspective of public good, to unlock the potential of data journalism would require news organisations to invest in additional, and unfamiliar, editorial resources. But doing so would go against the grain of the news industry over the last few years, as the push has been to reduce costs in newsrooms. From the perspective of news as a commodity, however, Big Data may afford media companies improved opportunities for revenue growth in at least two ways: first, through helping to streamline their business practices, and, second, through refining their understanding of audience and advertiser preferences when offering news products and services (Lewis and Westlund 2015).

Data Journalism in Ireland

Irish newspapers and broadcasters have been 'slow' to embrace data journalism, and much of the initial energy has been generated not by professional newsrooms but by independent bloggers (Lenihan 2015). This may be a symptom of the discomfort that data journalism causes to traditional newsmodels in Ireland, which have tended to place a higher value on reporting events and personalities than processes and long-term developments. Support for data journalism also requires ambition, innovation, and investment at a time when, in the context of a small but highly globalised domestic media market, Irish news organisations have been experiencing tough trading conditions. Figures from industry representative group News Brands Ireland could be considered to be an industry lobby group, but I want to avoid using that term because of its negative connotations (NBI 2015). In the same period, the market value of print and broadcast advertising in Ireland has also declined significantly, with growth in digital advertising being too low to compensate (Indecon 2014).

The dominant players in Ireland's news market are the public service broadcaster RTE and the legacy newspaper publisher Independent News and Media (INM). Neither organisation has developed a significant profile in data journalism. The resources available to RTE's newsroom have suffered through the downturn in advertising (which, alongside a licence fee, provides the bulk of the broadcaster's funding). INM, which publishes one of Ireland's most popular news websites, independent.ie, has adopted a 'digital first' editorial structure (INM 2015). However, this refers to the priority platform on which news content is published, not to a data-driven news agenda.

Newspaper and website publisher *The Irish Times* announced an initiative in early 2015 to 'put data journalism to the foreground' of the organisation's news offering (The Irish Times 2015). Irish Times Data highlighted the potential for data journalism to tell stories related to emigration, health, politics, and the economy in compelling and accessible formats. The production team makes its source data publicly available, but conceded that filtering and structuring data-sets and running visualisations was 'labour intensive' and required a range of journalistic and technical skills (The Irish Times 2015). Given the resource pressures squeezing Irish media organisations, the labour and technical costs associated with data journalism may be restricting its wider practice.

Globally, groups such as Open Knowledge have been campaigning for more transparent government and freer public access to the data sets that state institutions accumulate. Irish data journalism is developing in a legislative environment where Freedom of Information Act provisions are quite restrictive (Lenihan 2015). However, the government has made some efforts to increase public availability of data, notably through the establishment of Open Government Partnership Ireland (data.gov.ie) as a portal to the data sets of 85 state organisations and bodies. The facility is consistent with open government initiatives elsewhere, including the UK's portal at data.gov.uk. Internationally, organisations such as the World Bank, the World Health Organisation, and the European Union have been making extensive databanks publicly available.

CONCLUDING COMMENTS

Big Data itself is on the expanding list of social and technological complexities that the news-media is expected to explain to the public. Already, outlets such as *The Guardian* in the UK have provided vigorous coverage of Big Data's emergence and controversies, with a keen focus on the legitimacy of how state and corporate actors gather and use data on people's public and private activities. *The Guardian's title* is also a pioneer in the practice of data journalism in the UK. In these regards, the news organisation is applying its traditional informed-citizenry and watchdog roles to Big Data and is pushing the boundaries of data journalism innovation. Doing likewise in another of the world's larger and richer media markets, the USA, are *The New York Times*, *The Washington Post*, and the foundation-funded ProPublica.

Their efforts and achievements are the exception rather than the norm, however. Data journalism faces considerable challenges if it is to become a well-established, industry-supported genre of news. Like the implications of Big Data for the media generally, the challenges facing data journalism are not all apparent yet. But, at this stage, the transparency of externally-held data sets is a priority. To adequately extend their public service role to Big Data, news organisations will need greater knowledge of the data sets that state and corporate actors possess and why they possess them (including the configuration of the algorithms processing the data). Further, news organisations will require formal and accountable mechanisms to access state-held data sets when it is appropriate and necessary to do so in the public interest.

A challenge internal to the news industry hinges on data journalism gaining wider acceptance and support amongst news professionals. Since the late nineteenth century, journalists' professional expectations have developed around notions of news being *about* people, produced by speaking *to* people. This 'social practice' of journalism is a far cry from the technical task of interrogating patterns across multiple data sets (Carlson 2015, p. 417). Warming to the idea of data as news will, for many journalists, take time. Further, and resonating with the discussion in Zwitter's contribution to this volume, news media organisations will need to refresh and perhaps redraw the ethical frameworks and professional guidelines underpinning their corporate and editorial behaviour in an increasingly data-driven and networked world. Another challenge stems from the commercial structures of news production, which are calibrated to attract audiences and advertisers. To receive robust industry support, data journalism will need to justify itself as an informational commodity. To this point, arguably, the public good value of data journalism is more evident than its commercial value.

References

Anderson, C. W. (2015). Between the unique and the pattern: Historical tensions in our understanding of quantitative journalism. *Digital Journalism, 3*(3), 349–363.

Briggs, A., & Burke, P. (2005). *A social history of the media: From Gutenberg to the internet*. Cambridge: Polity Press.

Carlson, M. (2015). The robotic reporter: Automated journalism and the redefinition of labour, compositional forms, and journalistic authority. *Digital Journalism, 3*(3), 416–431.

Cole, P., & Harcup, T. (2010). *Newspaper journalism: Key texts*. London: Sage.

Doyle, G. (2006). Financial news journalism: A post-enron analysis of approaches towards economic and financial news production in the UK. *Journalism, 7*(4), 433–452.

Fahy, D. (2014). A limited focus? Journalism, politics and the Celtic Tiger. In M. O'Brien & D. O'Beachain (Eds.), *Political communication in the Republic of Ireland* (pp. 129–146). Liverpool: Liverpool University Press.

Franklin, B. (2014). The future of journalism. *Journalism Studies, 15*(5), 481–499.

Gandy, O. (1982). *Beyond agenda setting: Information subsidies and public policy*. New York: Ablex.

Independent News and Media. (2014). Annual Report. Retried April 4, 2016, from http://inmplc.com/news/uploads/INM_Annual_Report_2014_for_web.pdf

Indecon. (2014). Economic analysis of the advertising market in Ireland 2013. Retrieved July 9, 2015, from http://www.dcenr.gov.ie/NR/rdonlyres/D5003758-B55B-446B-985C-6A131369B3D2/0/EconomicAnalysis ofAdvertisingMarketIndeconReport.pdf

Lenihan, H. (2015). Digital journalism: Reinventing news for 21st century. Retrieved July 7, 2015, from http://www.irishtimes.com/opinion/data-journalism-reinventing-news-for-21st-century-digital-society-1.2119160

Lewis, S., & Westlund, O. (2015). Big Data and journalism: Epistemology, expertise, economics and ethics. *Digital Journalism, 3*(3), 447–466.

Lewis, J., Williams, A., & Franklin, B. (2008). A compromised fourth estate? *Journalism Studies, 9*(1), 1–20.

Lippmann, W. (2009). *The phantom public*. New Jersey: Transaction Publishers.

News Brands Ireland. (2015). Retrieved July 9, 2015, from http://newsbrandsireland.ie/data-centre/circulation/

O'Brien, M. (2015). The Irish press, politicians, and the Celtic Tiger economy. In S. Schifferes & R. Roberts (Eds.), *The media and financial crisis: Comparative and historical perspectives* (pp. 75–86). New York: Routledge.

Parasie, S. (2015). Data-driven revelation? Epistemological tensions in investigative journalism in the age of 'Big Data'. *Digital Journalism, 3*(3), 364–380.

Parasie, S., & Dagiral, E. (2013). Data-driven journalism and the public good: 'Computer-assisted-reporters' and 'programmer-journalists' in Chicago. *New Media and Society, 15*(6), 853–871.

Sinclair, U. (2003). *The brass check: A study of American journalism.* Urbana and Chicago: University of Illinois Press.

Tambini, D. (2010). What are financial journalists for? *Journalism Studies, 11*(2), 158–174.

The Irish Times. (2015). Welcome to Irish Times data. Retrieved July 7, 2015, from http://www.irishtimes.com/news/ireland/irish-news/welcome-to-irish-times-data-1.2089414

PART II

Implications for Security

Sustainable Innovation: Placing Ethics at the Core of Security in a Big Data Age

Michael Mulqueen

Abstract This chapter explores the broader security implications of the Big Data age. To what extent should state agencies make decisions on the basis of no other evidence than algorithmic sorting of messy, raw data? And how do these agencies marry innovation with ethics in order to prevent blowback from the media and public? Michael Mulqueen raises pertinent ethical problems and addresses the need for professional ethics in organisations working on security. It is argued that decisions to deploy Big Data are being made in the absence of any systematic epistemology or methodology to track and manage the influences of human intuition and social processes on that action.

Keywords Big Data • Algorithmic security • Intelligence agencies • Military intelligence • Geopolitics of data • Global surveillance • Ethics • Innovation • Virtuous organisation • Sustainable innovation

Introduction: Shakespeare and the Sniper

A year from now, a 22-year-old platoon commander is positioned with his troops one kilometre outside of a village from which, hours beforehand, enemy forces have reportedly withdrawn. Standard operating procedure

M. Mulqueen (✉)
Leicestershire Police, Leicester, UK

© The Editor(s) (if applicable) and The Author(s) 2016
A. Bunnik et al. (eds.), *Big Data Challenges*,
DOI 10.1057/978-1-349-94885-7_6

61

dictates that he orders a selection of his troops into the village to conduct reconnaissance and confirm the absence of hostiles. This is one of the most demanding burdens on the shoulders of a young commander—to place young soldiers in harm's way. And for what ends? Intelligence is, after all, only an educated guess. Reconnaissance, for all of its costs in spilt blood, frequently provides but a partial picture. He reaches instead for a combat infantry specification laptop and, from it, in a few minutes of purposeful clicking, draws down analytics on the primary threat to the safety of his men. The data shows, to a very high probability, that, over the last five years, the withdrawing enemy has tactically deployed snipers in villages shaped just like this one. The numbers suggest that the 'bad guys' tend to shoot at sunset on west-facing streets that intersect the main roads and from houses with skylights providing both cover and a wide, lethal arc of fire. A double check on Google Maps verifies that, in the village before him, there is only one such road and one such house on it. In all likelihood—the logic of data tells him—this is where a sniper is awaiting his men. So the commander faces a choice: does he risk the lives of his men on a mission the success of which will be defined as much by the luck of their guesswork as their survival, or does he act on the data before him with decisive, deadly force? A surveillance drone flight proves inconclusive. So, he calls instead for an armed drone strike. His men are shielded from unavoidable risk and no civilian is caught in the crossfire with a sniper. But by directing a pre-emptive strike against a civilian building on the basis of no other evidence than algorithmic sorting of messy, raw data, has he just turned himself into a war criminal (and killed a family inside)?

In 2013, Ewan Birney, a respected scientist at the European Molecular Biology Laboratory (EMBL)-European Bioinformatics Institute (EMBL-EBI), chatted amiably on BBC Radio 4's 'The Life Scientific' programme about his pioneering work on deciphering the human genome and junk DNA. The conversation between Birney and presenter Jim Al-Khalili turned to an idea spawned over pints, after a long day's work, in a pub in Hamburg. The challenge conceived amongst Birney's colleagues that night was to scientifically identify a storage material robust enough to carry the vast quantities of data coming down the line for humanity. Back in the laboratory, they went on to demonstrate that artificial DNA was that material. On a tiny speck they loaded a large data chunk, namely Shakespeare's sonnets saved in PDF form. 'One gram of DNA can store two petabytes of information,' Birney confirmed, before musing how this breakthrough could allow all of the world's data to be stored in a single room. Rather excitedly, interviewer and interviewee agreed that a test tube might soon replace a hard drive (BBC 2013). But Birney's team may have opened the door on something altogether more profound. Given that we have established artificial DNA to be a highly efficient means of storage, can we reach the point of similarly harnessing natural, human DNA? Do we face the vista of loading information on the human, wiping information from the human, re-loading altered information, and so on? There may be a great deal of good in society's having such ability. But where might this leave the capacity to trust? Alarming questions would arise for security and intelligence gathering based on human sources, the reliability of evidence at trial, and, indeed, any facet of societal activity predicated on the repository we call human memory. It may be that the only obstacle standing in the way to these extraordinary shifts is the pace of scientific endeavour—and laboratory ethics.

ETHICS AND INNOVATIONS IN BIG DATA

The purpose of this chapter is not to decry Big Data. To do so would be unhelpful on two fronts. First, it would be to ignore Big Data's huge potential as a driver for innovation. Second, given Big Data's penetration in decision-making in public and private organisations, it would be like seeking to roll back history or like using a Popsicle stick to dam a river's flood. Rather—and as this book seeks to point out—the implications of Big Data, as with any powerful tool, need to be thought through by its users and managers lest the quest for its advantages turns out to be a journey into nightmare. The points made here are not, in the main, written by data scientists. The text is not a highway to the miraculous technical solution that will rule out blowback from Big Data. Instead, what is offered is the insight of authors who are expert in how organisational decisions are made in the public policy process, including national security, and in the security industry. It is written as Big Data is starting to have a serious impact on government and business and as the world experiences the first major indicators of the scale of trouble Big Data can cause when the structures to manage it are immature. The argument of this chapter is that, when an organisation creates a robust, systematic interplay between innovation and ethics, the innovations derived from Big Data will be more likely to be sustained and less likely to cause blowback. Sustainable innovation maximises the yield whilst managing the risks. The required interplay needs to take place at all levels of the organisation. The goals are innovation by the many and not just the few, and innovation with ethics to generate profit and well being, the approach of the virtuous organisation.

The global controversy that blew up with the data leaks to the media by US National Security Agency (NSA) contractor Edward Snowdon demonstrated the potential of Big Data to backfire against national security policy and industry. This potential is explored here along several fronts: Big Data threatens to accelerate a return, arguably already underway, to great-power rivalry in international politics. Big Data is raising corporate risk for public and private organisations; these risks include customer hostility when the significance of information is missed (for example, law enforcement or publicly quoted companies) or 'too much' information is acquired or stolen. Another is the financial costs when the systems using the data go down. Big Data enterprise, such as click advertising, as well as data-driven national intelligence are vulnerable to widespread public perceptions of ethical failure in data gathering and processing. A useful example is venture capital investment in privacy technologies grows, at least partially, from a failure in ethics driving a market for privacy which, in turn, makes data access more difficult. The importance of living in a corporate culture that is ethically tuned to Big Data is clear when employees, perceiving them as unethical, turn on their organisations. They may release sensitive information in reprisal or do worse. Such instances may have measurable impacts on shareholder confidence, public trust, bottom line, organisational morale, innovation, and sustainability.

GEOPOLITICS: DATA AS THE NEW OIL?

Let us begin with geopolitics. Much of the world's information is carried by fibre optic cable and most cabling traverses the Atlantic seabed.[1] Each cable reportedly carries data at a rate of 10 gigabits per second or a theoretical maximum of 21 petabytes a day. The *Guardian* estimated this capability as the equivalent of sending all of the information in all of the books in the British Library 192 times every 24 hours (MacAskill et al. 2013). The significance of the cables to national security crystallised with newspaper revelations of Operation Tempora, run by Britain's signals intelligence agency, Government Communications Headquarters (GCHQ), to access user metadata from the web. Documents leaked to *The Guardian* by Snowden suggested that, in 2012, GCHQ handled 600 million 'telephone events' each day, tapped more than 200 fibre optic cables, and was able to process data from at least 46 of them' (MacAskill et al. 2013). Tempora, which the UK's Investigatory Powers Tribunal (IPT) subsequently found to be lawful, existed in addition to Prism, whereby the NSA reportedly secured access to the internal systems of global companies servicing the internet, and surveillance programs like OAKSTAR, STORMBREW, BLARNEY, and FAIRVIEW, which, apparently, functioned similarly to Tempora (Khazan 2013).

Perhaps understandably, much of the political and media focus during the subsequent controversy fell upon the extent to which the public's privacy was breached in a wholesale manner and the degree to which the law upheld this breach. Less prominent was a sense of how the revelations suggested the strategic value of information, now that sufficient processing power and storage existed to refine its immense potential: comparisons with crude oil appear apt (Arthur 2013). Also missed was the intrinsic importance to future strategic calculations of the cables used to transit information from destination to destination. Interrupt these for a prolonged period and, perhaps, economies may suffer. When Google went offline for four minutes in August 2013, it was estimated that the missed chance to show advertisements to searchers cost $500,000 (Arthur 2013). The controversy has, therefore, underlined what analysts have opined for some time: fibre optic cables are comparable to pipelines carrying oil and may be just as likely to cause international tension, if not conflict.

For states and the defence industry alike, the capacity of protecting cable and cable infrastructure is a serious business, and the geographical clustering of cables matters. Cable entry or exit east or west of the Atlantic is likely to be the concern of NATO or NATO-friendly naval forces and, as such, a comparatively stable proposition. But stability in this context is a function of many things, not the least of which is continued reliance on the same cables. Data growth is occurring at such pace and quantity that today's cables, as impressive as their capacities appear now, will be dwarfed by a next generation, whose location in the oceans of the world may not be the choice of states but of the corporations which own them. There is an incentive for states who seek to rival western powers to strike attractive terms with such companies and, therefore, effectively move the trade lanes of information within their spheres of influence and sovereign waters.

The information race need not be limited to the maritime domain, however. Especially in developing markets with immature but growing communications architecture, the opportunity for corporations, including those closely aligned with states, to penetrate the market with technologies that both disperse and generate user data (for example, cell phones) is obvious.[2] Intricate inter-corporation deals, covering everything from subcontracting of parts supply to servicing, create confusing opacity over who is collecting and storing what, where, and how. Yet, the data generated, while useful for profit and influence, has no finite shelf life. Therefore, and at an altogether deeper level of consequence, what it tells us about ourselves now may shape our self-perception in the future. Those who own the data can shape the data we receive and, therefore, the datafied world in which we exist and perceive. It cuts to the DNA of the very ideas we think we devise. But, for now, let us encounter this problem of lives lived in such data bubbles by thinking in terms of the creation of a discourse of national security. Useful here is Barry Buzan's concept of the 'binding idea of the state' or the notion that binds the citizenry to the state and keeps it loyal despite the state's exercise of security at the expense of personal freedom (Buzan 1991). Where the binding is too weak, the public will reject the state and its security. Where it is too strong, the binding idea is no less dangerous; Germany after 1933 is an often-cited example.

These suggestions and scenarios may imply that the inclination towards ethical behaviour in Big Data is naïve or even dangerous. But there are solid grounds for adopting an approach of enlightened self-interest. Big Data can do a great many things. Let us consider Big Data as a force multiplier for navies and a source of efficiencies for the burdened taxpayers. One senior European Union (EU) naval officer proposed using data from two decades of fisheries patrols to identify where illegal fisheries will probably take place a week before his ships deploy (author's interview). Similar gains can be imagined in respect to seaborne narcotics smuggling and human trafficking. Such imagining of new possibilities and the delivery of the technology to turn aspiration into reality reflect the innovative mind at work. Indeed, as leading innovation thinker Eric von Hippel of MIT's Sloan School of Management argues, users—such as our naval officer—are a powerful source of innovation (von Hippel 1994). The challenge is to harness innovation without losing sight of ethics.

The reasons offered are all to do with practical implications and the bottom line. The morning after Edward Snowden stepped forward as the person who leaked information about the NSA's surveillance programmes, shares in his employer, Booz Allen Hamilton Corporation, dropped 4 per cent (72 cents to $17.28) (The Associated Press 2013). Booz Allen Hamilton has, for many years, provided management and consulting services to the US government, particularly the defence and intelligence agencies, from its Beltway base in McLean, Virginia. The company has thousands of intelligence analysts, including technologists such as Snowdon, under contract to the US government. Profitable and well capitalised, it was bought by the Carlyle Group for $2.54 billion in 2008 amid the US recession (Heath and Censer 2013). In 2012, about

23% of its revenue, or $1.3 billion, came from US intelligence agencies (The Associated Press 2013). By way of an indicator of scale, the US government budget for classified and other secret operations for the 16 agencies comprising the intelligence community in the 2013 fiscal year was $53 billion (United States of America: Office of the Director of National Intelligence 2013, p. 1). Various Booz Allen Hamilton contractors need to achieve security clearance to a level where they can access classified and other secret government information. Recognising this, the company warned in its filings to the US Securities and Exchange Commission that security breaches could materially hurt it (The Associated Press 2013). And within weeks of Snowden's flight to Moscow, reports came through from its subcontractors—small companies depending upon the Booz Allen mother ship—that it was losing business and cancelling contracts as a result. The Snowden saga was, so the word went, starting to hurt client-customer trust, bottom-line profitability, and, most seriously of all, jobs, even if the sector has subsequently recovered.

Many criticisms are made of the labyrinthine contracting system operating within the Washington, DC, beltway. However, contracting has in its favour a likely reduction in labour costs to government and may make available to policy managers a wider pool of skilled problem solvers. But an important lesson from Booz Allen Hamilton is that employees who perceive their organisations to be innovating in a less-than-ethical way may take it upon themselves to harm the company and, in this case, the state for which it was working. Good corporate strategy, therefore, demands that ethics is not only high on the agenda but part of the organisation's actions at all levels.

Market reaction to Big Data privacy scandals concerns business as well as government. In the USA in 2012, venture capitalists invested $700 million in security start-ups, according to Lawrence Pingree of Gartner Inc., the US information technology research company, in an interview with the *Wall Street Journal* (Nissenbaum 2013). By the same measure, however, where large numbers of internet users become sensitised to surveillance, investors will chase opportunities in privacy. As Pingree put it, 'Money always follows problems' (Nissenbaum 2013). Perceptions of trust are critical here. Until very recently, Big Data was all about mathematics and smart infrastructure to manipulate it. An effect of Snowden was to remove the Big Data world from its laboratory-like conditions and drop it deep into the messiness of human impression and sentiment. So, it may matter to the market that the Hadoop-based Accumulo database—although now in commercial form as an open source project—started life in the NSA and apparently remains it primary data store and analysis engine (Harris 2013). The challenge for a developer or an organisation vulnerable to being caught in this bind is the importance of being perceived as trustworthy and ethical in the marketplace. Being on the side of the angels makes sound business sense. This is especially so in the security industry, where, invariably, companies and organisations 'on the side of the state' will be held in suspicion. Hence, the decisions of such companies to make use of Big Data must be put through a purpose-built ethical framework.

Ethics mitigate corporate risk. The corporate risks from Big Data extend beyond being left high and dry as the market moves towards privacy. Vast quantities of data floating about constitute a problem in themselves. Some estimates suggest the world contains about 8 zettabytes (ZB) of data (one ZB = 1 billion terabytes), the vast majority created in the last five years (Arthur 2013). Law enforcement and national security agencies are rightly worried. At a recent Global Intelligence Forum in Dungarvan, Ireland, run by Mercyhurst University's Institute of Intelligence, senior transnational intelligence analysts wondered aloud about the boundaries of the data they could search. Put another way, seasoned practitioners are looking for ethical and legal limitations to avoid future crisis. Another line of concern for senior national security managers, who failed to act on it, was the latent political and public risk waiting to be triggered should it be discovered that information was available to the authorities through Big Data. That the information could be a tiny signal in a mass of (messy data) noise would not matter in the media and political cacophony.

One can trace a clear link to the problem of holding the data to the lightning speed of data processing: in 2012, between 50% and 70% of all trades on US stock exchanges were done by machines which could carry out a transaction in less than a microsecond (millionth of a second). Is it ethical and wise to leave decision-making about trades—much less national security—solely to hyper-fast machinery? Where, without 'slow thinking,' is there room for human intuition and the subtlety of context made explicit by social theory? There is no need, perhaps, for such accompaniment, save for the drastic consequences that lie in store from an unbridled regime of hyper-fast processing and messy raw-source data (Fig. 6.1). The 143-points drop in Wall Street prices triggered instantly by a corrupted Twitter feed suggesting that the White House had been bombed is a sobering wake-up call of what can happen to revenues (and reputations) when humanity is removed from the warp speed data cycle (Arthur 2013).

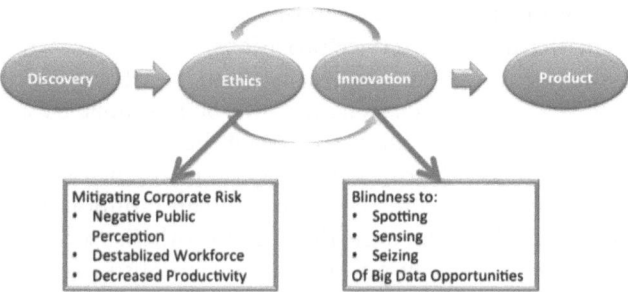

Fig. 6.1 Ethics and innovation in Big Data product design

Conclusions

This chapter argues that innovation without ethics in Big Data is unsustainable. This argument is not the bleating of out-of-touch academics. As far back as July 2012, one of the main takeaways to emerge from a Policy Exchange/EMC Greenplum event in London was—rather hopefully—that the UK should bring forward a code for responsible analytics. As mentioned above, practitioners at the Global Intelligence Forum spoke out about the want of limitations on what they can do. The issue is not only the range of data which can be mined, stored, and analysed, but the speed at which processing can take place. In their influential study of Cuban Missile Crisis decision-making, Graham Allison and Philip Zelikow spoke of the pressure on players to, as they put it, 'say something, anything' to stay relevant to the decision (Allison and Zelikow 1999). Amid the mighty torque of Big Data findings, any kind of human voice is a challenge. Human absence is a risk when we trust machines to make major calls using data which, at times, is dangerously messy. Part of the problem is the way Big Data fits the descriptor 'known unknown'. Its progress is racing ahead of the usual social checks, such as law, ethics, and social science theory, on scientific progress. Decisions to deploy Big Data are being made in the absence of any systematic epistemology or methodology to track and manage the influences of human intuition and social processes on that action. The literature and accompanying knowledge-transfer infrastructure simply do not exist. Yet, the world faces geostrategic uncertainty in the infrastructure of Big Data (for example, its cabling), and serious questions can be asked as to the power and influence vested in next-generation 'information is power' brokers, including Google, Amazon, and others mastering cloud-service provisions. Business and government can hardly avoid blowback when flying so blind. In the face of such a challenging outlook for public trust, customer loyalty, and reputational brand, we advocate the following. In any organisation, a state of maturity in Big Data use can be reached when humanity is brought back centrally into the cycle. Human intuition is the essence of innovation that drives forward the data hypothesis; social theory tells us how far we can ethically go. This is not an abstract proposition; a virtuous-organisation approach includes models and processes that can be applied to real-world organisational challenges, and can be learned. Innovation without ethics is a road to ruin. Ethics without innovation is stasis. Between idea and product in Big Data comes successful interplay between innovation and ethics. This Big Data progress is more likely to be sustainable and a better investment.

NOTES

1. For a useful map of undersea fibre-optic cables see http://cdn.theatlantic. com/static/mt/assets/international/Screen%20Shot%202013-07-16%20 at%2011.17.56%20AM.png
2. As an example of growing scale, consider Chinese smartphone maker Xiamoi, which overtook Apple's iPhone in China within 3 years and claims a valuation of $10bn in August 2013, up from $4bn in June 2012. It has announced plans to double handset sales to 15 m per year. A $10bn valuation compares to a market value, in August 2013, of $10bn for Lenovo, the world's biggest PC maker, and about $20bn for Sony Corporation (Bloomberg News 2013).

REFERENCES

Allison, G., & Zelikow, P. (1999). *Essence of decision: Explaining the Cuban Missile Crisis* (2nd ed.). New York: Pearson.

Arthur, C. (2013, August 3). Tech giants may be huge, but nothing matches big data. *The Guardian*. Retrieved September 1, 2013, from http://theguardian. com/technology/2013/aug/23/tech-giants-data

BBC. (2013, June 11). The life scientific. *BBC Radio 4* [online]. Retrieved August 28, 2013, from http://www.bbc.co.uk/programmes/p01b84wv

Bloomberg News. (2013, August 23). Xiaomi director says valuation reaches $10 billion. *Bloomberg* [online]. Retrieved August 26, 2013, from www.bloomberg. com/news/2013-08-23/xiaomi-director-says-valuation-reaches-10-billion.html

Buzan, B. (1991). *People, states and fear: An agenda for international security studies in the post-Cold War era* (2nd ed.). Hemel Hempstead: Harvester Wheatsheaf.

Harris, D. (2013, August 22). Big Data is a bubble? Don't tell that to these guys. *Gigaom* [online]. Retrieved August 26, 2013, from www.gigaom. com/2013/08/22/big-data-is-a-bubble-dont-tell-that-to-these-guys

Heath, T., & Censer, M. (2013). NSA revelations put Booz Allen Hamilton, Carlyle Group in uncomfortable limelight [online]. Retrieved June 11, 2013, from http://articles. washingtonpost.com/2013-06-11/business/39896957_1_carlyle-group-nsa-firm

Khazan, O. (2013, July 16). The creepy, long-standing practice of undersea cable tapping. *The Atlantic* [online]. Retrieved August 29, 2013, from http://www. theatlantic.com/international/archive/2013/07/the-creepy-long-standing-practice-of-undersea-cable-tapping/277855/

MacAskill, J., Borger, J., Hopkins, N., Davies, N., & Ball, J. (2013, June 21). GCHQ taps fibre-optic cables for secret access to world's communications. *The Guardian* [online]. Retrieved August 29, 2013, from http://www.theguardian.com/uk/2013/jun/21/gchq-cables-secret-world-communications-nsa

Nissenbaum, D. (2013, July 22). Venture funds invest in electronic spying startups. *Wall Street Journal* [online]. Retrieved August 31, 2013, from http://online. wsj.com/article/SB10001424127887324263404578612232678888390.html

The Associated Press. (2013, June 10). Booz Allen Hamilton shares shed 4% after NSA leak news [online]. Retrieved August 30, 2013, from http://www.nbcnews.com/ business/booz-allen-hamilton-shares-shed-4-after-nsa-leak-news-6C10262985

United States of America: Office of the Director of National Intelligence. (2013). National Intelligence Programme Summary: FY2013 Congressional Budget Justification, Vol. 1 [online]. Retrieved August 30, 2013, from http://apps.washingtonpost. com/g/page/national/inside-the-2013-us-intelligence-black-budget/420/

Von Hippel, E. (1994). *The sources of innovation*. USA: Oxford University Press.

CHAPTER 7

Needles in Haystacks: Law, Capability, Ethics, and Proportionality in Big Data Intelligence-Gathering

Julian Richards

Abstract As we move resolutely into a Big Data age, it appears that a sense of 'panoptic panic', boosted by the Snowden revelations, about the expanding capabilities of our intelligence agencies is growing amongst sections of the public. Law enforcers and security officials will often speak about the need to amass large amounts of data to find needles in haystacks, but civil libertarians and cyber-utopianists warn of a slide towards Orwellian powers of mass surveillance. Big Data implies an epistemological shift in data analysis, and opens up new opportunities for security agencies to become more proactive and pre-emptive. This chapter argues that, while the risks of such a move must be recognised, we must also be able to deliver security responsibly.

Keywords Big Data • Intelligence agencies • Snowden revelations • Global surveillance • Ethics of intelligence • Law enforcement • Intelligence-led policing • Intelligence-gathering • Risk society

J. Richards (✉)
Centre for Intelligence and Security Studies (BUCSIS),
University of Buckingham, Buckingham, UK

© The Editor(s) (if applicable) and The Author(s) 2016   73
A. Bunnik et al. (eds.), *Big Data Challenges*,
DOI 10.1057/978-1-349-94885-7_7

INTRODUCTION

Edward Snowden's revelations in 2013 about the nature and scale of data-gathering in the two intelligence agencies the National Security Agency (NSA) in the USA and its UK sister agency, the Government Communications Headquarters (GCHQ), added a new dimension to a debate already underway about the transformation of intelligence-gathering in a Big Data age. There is no doubt that Snowden's disclosures provided the bow-wave of a fundamentally critical and anti-state stance on the intelligence questions in hand. Such a critical stance is reflected in much of the academic literature about Big Data. This chapter critically appraises such concerns.

The core theme in much of the critical discourse is that of the 'panoptic panic' described by Lyon (2014 p. 6), in which the citizens of liberal democracies increasingly feel threatened by the descent of their societies into an Orwellian dystopia of 'mass surveillance' (itself a contested notion, about which more below). There is a sense of creeping anxiety to match the supposedly creeping powers of state intelligence-gatherers, and increasingly sophisticated techniques can become more pre-emptive and predictive in their stance, with all the attendant risks of misdiagnosis of miscreants and leading to wrongful imprisonment, or worse. We are moving, say the critics, into the sort of 'pre-crime' nightmare that has been the realm of movies hitherto ('Minority Report', 'Robocop'), to say nothing of the risks of a state's abusing its increasingly powerful capabilities for political or corrupt purposes. Such risks are diametrically opposed to the liberating hopes of the cyber-utopianists of Silicon Valley in the 1990s, exemplified by such writers as Barlow (1996), whose ultra-libertarian notions of cyberspace posed an explicit challenge to supposedly repressive regimes and the states of the real world. Such libertarian ideology spawned the likes of Edward Snowden, Julian Assange of WikiLeaks, and numerous others.

At the core of the critical debate is the perennial question about the balancing of security against freedom in a modern liberal democracy. As transnational threats such as organised crime and terrorism take root, might we become a paranoid 'risk society', in Ulrich Beck's conceptualisation (Beck 2002)? As the state capitalises on sophisticated data-gathering and data-modelling opportunities, are we doing the work of the enemies of democracy for them by turning full circle into a Stasi-like surveillance society? In Beck's analysis, prediction and risk are interrelated concepts:

fear of the latter leads to an increasing desire for capability in the former and to attempts to block risks before they happen (Kerr and Earle 2013, p. 68). Such fundamental questions about the desired nature of modern democratic society could hardly be more important, and Big Data may be posing new and particularly challenging questions in the debate.

EPISTEMOLOGICAL ISSUES

Much of the academic discussion in this area grapples with the epistemological shift that Big Data supposedly demands. Big Data is not just about handling data in traditional ways but at much greater volumes. Instead, normative thinking suggests that Big Data opens up a whole new set of techniques and capabilities which move data analysis away from a retrospective building of links between entities and towards more pre-emptive and predictive possibilities. The whole paradigm of analysis and its outcomes starts to be redefined.

In the criminal intelligence sphere, such possibilities were noted relatively early in the 1990s in the shape of 'intelligence-led policing', which evolved into 'predictive policing'. Here, the idea was that data could be used much more intelligently to focus and direct increasingly pressured surveillance and interdiction resources by modelling criminal patterns spatially and temporally. These, in turn, could be used to predict future crime activities and patterns. In a world of public sector cutbacks, the dividends could be significant.

The concept made perfect sense, although subsequent experience has shown this process to be more difficult than it initially seemed. At the root of the problem may be a cultural issue within Western policing, whereby senior managers schooled in traditional, pre-information-age techniques for tackling crime have not yet understood the potential offered by manipulation of data for intelligence benefits (with some honourable exceptions). For some of these managers, data analysis produces little more than pretty pictures and maps to adorn mandated strategic crime reports.

As metropolitan societies moved resolutely into the information age and the twenty-first century, with its seemingly exponential rise in available data and the possibilities for analysing it, the debate intensified, This explosion in data is being matched by substantial developments in computing power and in the ability of states and organisations not only to store more data, but to run highly sophisticated analytical techniques against it. In policing and in intelligence, the possibilities of predictive policing are being reappraised.

Of course we now know through Snowden's revelations that the big signals intelligence (Sigint) agencies on either side of the Atlantic were working away throughout this period to capitalise on the new opportunities and to expand to the very limits of computing capability. At the heart of the revelations is the question of the scale of data-gathering. In the USA, the newly exposed Prism programme revealed an industrial-scale collection of internet metadata from major commercial internet service providers. Meanwhile, across the Atlantic, the Tempora programme revealed that GCHQ was tapping into trunk trans-global fibre optic cables transiting its shores in order to amass enormous databases of international communications activity.

There is a two-pronged question here of the intelligence rationale being adopted by the USA and the UK (and, undoubtedly, by numerous other states). First, and perhaps more significant, is the way in which national security conceptualisation and policy have changed through the turn of the century, particularly in the post-Cold War and post-9/11 era. The terrorist attacks in the USA in September 2001 ushered in the War on Terror, and, with it, an avowedly more pre-emptive and offensive-realist security stance in the USA and amongst its closest Western allies. President Bush's first State of the Union address after the attacks captured the mood:

> I will not wait on events, while dangers gather. I will not stand by, as peril draws closer and closer… We can't stop short. If we stop now–leaving terror camps intact and terror states unchecked–our sense of security would be false and temporary. History has called America and our allies to action, and it is both our responsibility and our privilege to fight freedom's fight. (CNN 2002)

From an intelligence-gathering perspective, such an avowedly more upstream approach is likely to mean two things. First, the supposedly transnational nature of threats like contemporary terrorism means that communications and connections between individuals and organisations will be made across global networks. It will not be enough, most probably, to restrict interception of communications to limited, domestic datasets, as such 'targets' and threats are likely to be operating in the civil sphere. The connection between terror camps in failed states and terrorist attackers in the Western world is likely to be embedded in particular civilian communities, whose communications will pass on public networks rather than in isolated and dedicated military or diplomatic channels, as might have been the case with targets of primary interest in the past.

If our states are to chase down such targets, therefore, they will need to dip their hands into public, civil communications, and data footprints. In former President Bush's terms, such a task was not just nice to have; rather, it was a matter of duty and responsibility, and a task of the loftiest importance, for the world's greatest power and its closest allies to 'fight freedom's fight'. Thus, the needs and values of democratic societies are balanced against the methods with which to deliver security. And the equation changed after 9/11. As the UK Prime Minister at the time, Tony Blair, described it, the attacks in New York and Washington had changed at a stroke the 'calculus of risk' (Richards 2012).

Needles and Haystacks

The second important component to the post-9/11 change in policy, however, is the methodology adopted to tackle the supposedly changed and enhanced threats posed in the new era. In this question, states could arguably be accused of using old thinking to tackle a new problem. Policing and intelligence organisations will often use the old analogy of searching for needles in haystacks. In contemporary society, it is assumed that a very small percentage of individuals is plotting to do us serious harm. But those individuals (and their planning) are lost within the vast morass of civil society. The trick is to find who they are and to extract them deftly from the welter of innocent citizens around them without disproportionately compromising democratic norms and expectations.

As communications behaviour expands and becomes more complex, however, the haystacks (that is, the data generated by modern citizens) start to become much bigger and diverse. Think of the way in which our communications behaviour has changed and the number of mechanisms we use on a daily basis to communicate. Not long ago, the fixed landline telephone was the only method of doing so. Now, many of us use a range of messaging applications for different purposes and different circles of people, with the applications sometimes numbering into double figures. For the intelligence agencies, each of these channels of communication is a potential new haystack in which the sought-after needles may be located.

A retrospective component seems to be at the centre of modern security threats in metropolitan societies. Intelligence agencies sometimes characterise this component as 'target discovery' or 'target development'. Perhaps not unreasonably, when a serious incident occurs, such as the bombing of Marathon runners in Boston or the attack on the Charlie

Hebdo magazine offices in Paris, the immediate question is whether the perpetrators were 'on the radar' of the security services. With depressing regularity, it usually transpires that the perpetrators were known to the authorities in some shape or form, but that investigations had not recognised the immediacy of the threat or prioritised counter-action.

The tactical and political challenge for such agencies in the wake of these incidents is twofold. First, there is the immediate tactical question of who else might be closely connected with the perpetrators and planners of this attack and possible future attacks. It appears that the only way we know how to find this out (a point to which I will return) is to quickly build the social networks of the perpetrators from available data not just pertaining to the aftermath of the attacks but also from the crucial pre-attack planning period. Doing so will allow the authorities to home in on and, possibly, arrest other suspects.

Big Data and sophisticated analytical techniques also offer the possibility of working horizontally rather than vertically, and reaching sideways into the discovery of other networks of individuals who are planning attacks but have not yet carried them out. It is assumed that groups planning criminal or terrorist activities interact with one another in especially covert and obscure ways so as to avoid the attention of the authorities. A specific and unusual pattern of communication such as an algorithm could be washed against the wider dataset of public communications to spot groups behaving in similar ways, creating the possibility of more preemptive and predictive intelligence analysis.

However, the critics pose this question: is the needle-in-a-haystack approach the wrong way of thinking about a new problem, especially if tackling the problem entails a massive intrusion into civil liberties through the collection of industrial-scale quantities of public communications data? The first question is whether mass 'collection' of data can be appropriately characterised as mass 'surveillance'. In much of the media and commentary about Snowden's revelations, data collection is often described as mass surveillance (see, for example, Lyon 2014, p. 3). Florid language suggests that new Big Data capabilities being proposed or exercised by the state allow for a panoptic nightmare in which unseen state officials sit in a room and examine each and every communication and interaction with the internet made by every man, woman, and child. In the UK, the Liberal Democrat MP Julian Huppert said of the proposed Data Communications Bill (defeated in the House of Lords on its first pass) that it would give 'huge powers to the Home Secretary to require information to be kept about every phone call you make, text you send, Facebook image you like, and anything else' (Huppert 2012). Connecting everyday activities with covert state surveillance is designed to emphasise the supposedly Orwellian and repressive nature of the modern state in a Big Data age. The French philosopher Gilles Deleuze suggested that there was no longer a difference between the toughest and most tolerant of regimes, since, within both, 'liberating and enslaving forces confront one another (1992, p. 4). The Foucauldian 'society of discipline' becomes the 'society of control'.

There are a number of risks identified by the critics. At the core of the argument is the basic question of 'proportionality' (to use the language of the European Convention on Human Rights), when a state appears to gather and store the vast majority of the public's communications, even if (as discussed below) a human eye never looks at more than a fraction of it. The fact is, it could be argued that the data has been gathered and public privacy compromised. Furthermore, as Lyon (2014 p. 9) suggests, '[t]he needle-and-haystack argument carries with it a high probability of false positives, which do matter immediately and intensely because the likelihood is high of harm to specific persons.'

The second risk of the needle-and-haystack approach is, therefore, that either corruption or incompetence, neither of which is unknown in official milieux, could lead to the wrong person being criticised, arrested, or worse. Even in less dramatic circumstances, individuals could find their future employment prospects severely compromised if they found themselves on the 'wrong list', even if the listing happened many years ago. Similarly, insurance could become costly or even unattainable.

We can think here of the case of Lotfi Raissi, the Algerian flight instructor who was the first person to be arrested in connection with the 9/11 attacks. Information subsequently revealed that basic social network analysis, in which Raissi had been in communication with most of the 9/11 hijackers, sealed his fate as a suspect. After many months in gaol and the threat of dire consequences if the US managed to extradite him from London where he had been arrested, Raissi sued the government for wrongful arrest and was awarded a six-figure sum in damages.

Part of the anxiety here arises from comparing commercial applications of Big Data analysis to state security. We know that major corporations are increasingly modelling consumer behaviour using large-scale data analysis to good commercial effect. But the science is relatively untested at the time of writing, and there are instances of things going wrong. The case of Google Flu Trends is an interesting one. Here, data derived from search terms entered into Google was used to predict the spread of influenza in the USA. Despite successful earlier analysis, the 2013 modelling dramatically overestimated peak flu levels (Butler 2013). This error will probably lead to further refinement and development of the algorithm to ensure better performance rather than the scrapping of the whole approach. But the question could reasonably be asked as to whether the application of such techniques in a national security context could not sometimes lead to more dire consequences for certain individuals and serious breaches of human rights. Do we know enough about these approaches yet to trust them in sensitive security contexts?

Zwitter (2014) argues that the questions posed by Big Data and its technological underpinnings may be outrunning the ethicists. If Big Data does indeed mean that intelligence-gathering is fundamentally changed by current developments, then ethical questions of what is right and wrong in a modern liberal democracy may have been thrown uncomfortably open. What, for example, does a rightful expectation of privacy mean in a world of comprehensive social networking?

The same dilemma could be said to apply to questions of law. In the UK, the parliamentary oversight committee, the Intelligence and Security Committee (ISC), has conducted a wide-ranging Privacy and Security Inquiry in the wake of the Snowden leaks. While this process has not yet been completed, one of its more substantive outcomes will likely be to suggest that the main law in the UK governing intelligence-gathering activities, the Regulatory and Investigatory Powers Act (RIPA), will need to be reviewed and overhauled, not least as it was drafted during the 1990s when modern internet-based communications were only beginning to emerge at scale.

The RIPA law allows for derogation from the relevant parts of the Human Rights Act (HRA) that govern the right to privacy under authorised activities where the interests of national security or threats of serious crime are relevant. Oversight of the government's activities in these areas is provided by a set of independent commissioners (such as the Interception of Communications Commissioner), the ISC, and an Investigative Powers Tribunal (IPT) to which complaints of unlawfulness can be made by any member of the public.

As discussed, the government has also tried to put in place a Data Communications Bill, which would mandate communications service providers to store and make available on request communications data (that is, metadata rather than communications content) in support of intelligence operations. Following the defeat of this Bill in the House of Lords and in response to a European Court of Justice ruling that the 2009 Data Retention Directive was invalid, in 2014 the UK government passed emergency legislation called the Data Retention and Investigatory Powers Act (DRIPA) to address, the government said, problems of maintaining capability in the face of heightened threats to security from terrorism.

A number of critics have challenged the effectiveness of these oversight and legislative mechanisms in ensuring a proper balance between security and liberty. On the passing of DRIPA, fifteen leading technology law experts wrote the House of Commons an open letter that lamented a 'serious expansion of the British surveillance state,' which, they said, was in potential breach of European law (The Guardian 2014).

The defeated 2012 Data Communications Bill is regularly referred to as the 'Snooper's Charter' by critics. One of the leading critics, and the linchpin in opposition to the bill, is the former leader of the Liberal Democrats and Deputy Prime Minister, Nick Clegg. He has characterised opposition to the bill as being a problem of proportion. While he claims to support the need for strong security in the face of a changing threat, Clegg protests that 'it is not a very British thing to confer or imply guilt on the whole of the nation by retaining records of every website everyone has visited over the course of a year' (BBC 2015). Again, we see the notion that mass collection of data (and, in this case, metadata rather than the actual content of messages) compromises the human rights of the citizens of a modern liberal democracy, despite the protestations from the security services that they are merely amassing the haystacks so that they have a better chance of finding the needles. What is right or wrong here is an ethical question, but also a legal one in terms of defining and, indeed, updating the powers of the intelligence agencies.

It is also the case that the oversight mechanism in the UK is not necessarily trusted by all. *The Guardian*, one of the primary outlets for Snowden's leaks, was quick to point out that the Investigative Powers Tribunal's ruling against GCHQ in February 2015 for failing to make known to ministers the extent of its use of capabilities revealed by Snowden up to December 2014 was not only 'unlawful', but constituted the first ruling against an intelligence agency in the IPT's fifteen-year existence. Leaving aside asinine debates about the difference between the terms 'unlawful' and 'illegal' (despite repeated implications to the contrary in *The Guardian*, GCHQ has not yet been found to have broken any laws), it is clearly the case in much of the critical coverage of these issues that the ISC committee and the IPT lack credibility because they are seen as being part of the establishment.

CONCLUSIONS: COUNTERING THE CRITICS

In academic terms, the debates about the ethics of Big Data for intelligence-gathering are complex. It is probably fair to say that critical debates of the 'panoptic panic' kind are probably in the ascendant, bolstered by widespread media commentary from civil libertarians and cyber-utopianists. Underpinning the critical discourse is a fundamental distrust of state agencies to do the right thing ethically or legally, a view given extra impetus by the scale and breadth of some of the capabilities revealed by Snowden. The critics would probably argue that the state has the whip hand as it holds power and can operate in secret. Were it not for Snowden, argue the critics, none of this would have come to light.

It could be said, however, that there are some important counter-arguments to place before the critics. First, there is much evidence from those with an intimate working knowledge of how the intelligence agencies operate—including the ISC committee, for example—that operations are conducted with a scrupulous attention to proper authorisation and accountability. Certainly, the IPT's ruling against GCHQ was embarrassing and will cause questions to be asked amongst its management, but the fact remains that there has still been no evidence whatsoever that GCHQ has broken any law in any of its recent operations. One of its former directors, Sir David Omand, has written that compliance with the law has become firmly embedded in the agency's daily working culture (Omand 2012). While the ISC and IPT may be criticised for never, until very recently, delivering any verdict critical of the intelligence machinery, it is doing a disservice to the members of those bodies to suggest fundamental corruption in their activities. At the same time, bureaucracies do sometimes make mistakes.

The slippery and sometimes deliberate mutation in public discourse of large-scale collection of data into 'mass surveillance' is misleading and unhelpful. Certainly, there are reasonable questions to be asked about proportionality, and we should never lose sight in a liberal democracy of the risks of an erosion of our values in the face of creeping surveillance powers. But to suggest that the intelligence agencies are scrutinising each and every interaction we make on a daily basis and looking for 'thought-crimes' is fanciful if not ridiculous. Much evidence suggests that only a tiny proportion—less than one percent—of all collected data is ever reviewed by a human analyst. Such a comprehensive intrusion into privacy for such small returns may have pertinent ethical questions attached to it, but to suggest that these processes are akin to a reborn Stalinist Great Terror or Cultural Revolution is historically and morally inaccurate and inappropriate.

Part of the problem is a technical one: what is the best way to find the needles in the haystacks? Critics will point out that the traditional methods of collecting vast amounts of data are surely outmoded in an age of greatly enhanced analytical tools and capabilities. It must be possible to pinpoint targets of interest—when they need to be targeted—in much more focused ways that minimise collateral intrusion to the extent that Snowden has described.

However, experts and insiders will often suggest that there is, as yet, no known better way of finding targets within the morass of public communications. Furthermore, targets can often be found only through their connection with other key individuals as and when they surface. And retrospective analysis following target discovery is a critical part of the process. Without some form of data retention, it is difficult to see how discovery of the planning activities of newly emerging targets of interest can ever be achieved. Without using current techniques, how we could ever answer a question as to the circle of people that the Charlie Hebdo attackers came into contact with when they were planning their attacks? We would be able to look only to the next attack rather than try to pre-empt any nascent plans.

None of this is to say that new solutions, which may allow us to adopt less intrusive and more effective mechanisms of target discovery, to such problems will never be found. We cannot know what we do not yet know, and the pace at which computing technology is developing means that any predictions are unwise. In a sense, this is the promise and opportunity of Big Data: that it will not just give us more information, but will fundamentally change the way we think about and address such difficult questions.

REFERENCES

Barlow, J.P. (1996, February 8). A declaration of the independence of Cyberspace. *Davos*. Retrieved October 22, 2015, from https://projects.eff.org/~barlow/Declaration-Final.html

BBC. (2015, January 18). Nick Clegg defends opposition to 'snoopers' charter. Retrieved July 16, 2015, from http://www.bbc.co.uk/news/uk-politics-30870442

Beck, U. (2002). The terrorist threat: World risk society revisited. *Theory, Culture and Society, 19*(4), 39–55.

Butler, D. (2013). When Google got flu wrong. *Nature, 494*(7436), 155–156.

CNN. (2002). Bush State of the Union address. Retrieved July 17, 2015, from http://edition.cnn.com/2002/ALLPOLITICS/01/29/bush.speech.txt/

Deleuze, G. (1992). Postscript on the societies of control. *October, 59*, 3–7.

Huppert, J. (2012, December 11). Communications Data Bill cannot proceed. *Liberal Democrat Voice*. Retrieved July 17, 2015, from http://www.libdemvoice.org/julian-huppert-mp-writes-the-data-communications-bill-as-it-is-simply-cannot-proceed-32103.html

Kerr, I., & Earle, J. (2013). Prediction, preemption, presumption: How Big Data threatens big picture privacy. *Stanford Law Review Online, 66*(65).

Lyon, D. (2014, July–December). Surveillance, Snowden, and Big Data: Capacities, consequences, critique. *Big Data and Society*.

Omand, D. (2012). *Securing the state*. London: C. Hurst and Co.

Richards, J. (2012). *A guide to national security: Threats, responses and strategies*. Oxford: Oxford University Press.

The Guardian. (2014, July 15). Academics: UK 'Drip' data law changes are 'serious expansion of surveillance. Retrieved July 17, 2015, from http://www.theguardian.com/technology/2014/jul/15/academics-uk-data-law-surveillance-bill-rushed-parliament

Zwitter, A. (2014, July–December). Big Data ethics. *Big Data and Society*.

CHAPTER 8

Countering and Understanding Terrorism, Extremism, and Radicalisation in a Big Data Age

Anno Bunnik

Abstract Anno Bunnik explores the ramifications of Big Data for countering terrorism, extremism, and radicalisation. With the recent rise of jihadists and other extremists groups in the Middle East and Europe, how do state agencies respond through the use of Big Data? This chapter critically engages with questions such as the extent to which Big Data can inform us about and help prevent radicalisation. It deals with the role of non-governmental organisations and the private sector in this regard. Bunnik makes the argument that whilst it is inevitable that Big Data will take centre stage in counter-terrorism, its potential should also be utilised to better understand radicalisation and extremism.

Keywords Big Data • Terrorism • Counter-terrorism • Countering violent extremism • Radicalisation • Intelligence agencies • Intelligence gathering • Algorithmic security • Law enforcement • NGOs • Private sector • UK

A. Bunnik (✉)
Department of Media and Communication, Liverpool Hope University, Liverpool, UK

© The Editor(s) (if applicable) and The Author(s) 2016   85
A. Bunnik et al. (eds.), *Big Data Challenges*,
DOI 10.1057/978-1-349-94885-7_8

INTRODUCTION

The threat of terrorism and violent extremism has become one of the most pertinent security concerns of our time. Following the civil war in Syria and the rise of the Islamic State group, politicians and policymakers have widened and deepened a range of measures taken earlier during the 'War on Terror'. These policies centre on the interlinked notions of Counter-Terrorism (CT), Countering Violent Extremism (CVE), and radicalisation. In these developments, Big Data is increasingly taking centre stage. This chapter explores some of the opportunities and challenges of how Big Data relates to current strategies by European Union (EU) member states to tackle these security concerns. Specific attention is placed on the response in the UK.

COUNTER-TERRORISM AND COUNTERING VIOLENT EXTREMISM AND RADICALISATION

When dealing with terrorism, European states generally tend to strike a balance between so-called 'hard and soft measures'. Unlike certain states that place more emphasis on defeating terrorism through military means, such as the US-led military campaigns in Afghanistan and Iraq after 9/11, the EU and its member states often highlight the importance of strengthening the social fabric of society as a technique to counter support for terrorist groups (Council of the European Union 2005b). 'We do not believe it is possible to resolve the threats we face simply by arresting and prosecuting more people', argues the UK's Counter-Terrorism strategy (HM Government 2011, p. 11). The soft-power hypothesis holds that, through outreach to communities, governments can stop extremist movements from recruiting vulnerable youngsters. This outreach is partly socio-economic by creating job opportunities, and partly socio-political by addressing certain grievances, for instance, about the (mis)perception that the West is waging a war on Islam.

It is not just jihadists who pose a threat to European societies. Incidents of right-wing violence and terrorism have drawn the attention of security agencies and law enforcement. Anders Breivik, who executed the terrorist attack in Norway in 2011 that killed 77 people, springs to mind, as do more recent lone wolf attacks on Muslims, mosques, and refugee detention centres in EU countries. These developments have reaffirmed to policymakers that not just a radical interpretation of Islam can inspire people to commit violent acts, and even murder, but that violent extremism in general needs to be addressed (Council of the European Union 2005a, p. 2; HM Government 2015). For this reason, EU member states often invoke the notion of Countering Violent Extremism (CVE) in order to address the wider problem of violent extremism for pluralistic, liberal societies.

Policymakers in the EU and its member states have increasingly utilised the concept of 'radicalisation' to understand and address the pathway to terrorism. This concept tends to explain terrorism as a result of a more linear process in which an individual or network radicalises to the extent of committing violence. To this end, several months after a home-grown al Qaeda-inspired network carried out the London bombings, the EU Strategy for Combating Radicalisation and Recruitment to Terrorism (Council of the European Union 2005a) was adopted. The attacks may have been stopped if authorities had better monitored the radicalisation of these young men before their decision to target London's citizens. But liberal governments cannot monitor every suspected individual all the time without turning into a police state (for more on this delicate balancing act, see the chapter by Julian Richards) and potentially drive citizens away from the state as they no longer trust its intentions.

Counter-terrorism initiatives influenced by recent thinking on the notion of radicalisation include the EU-led Radicalisation Awareness Network (RAN), which facilitates regular meetings with law enforcement, social workers, academics, and Non-Governmental Organisations (NGOs) on topics such as 'policing', 'foreign fighters', and 'the Internet and Social Media'. This multi-actor approach creates issue-specific security networks between the public sector and partner organisations. In the UK, the national counter-terrorism strategy is called CONTEST and has a similar perspective on tackling terrorism. A main aspect of this programme is the Prevent-pillar, which seeks 'to stop people becoming terrorists or supporting terrorism' (HM Government 2011). The British strategy is designed to support so-called moderate voices and work together with educational institutions, social workers, the health sector, and other actors in direct contact with people who could be at risk for radicalisation. In some cases, those who are deemed at risk are referred to the Channel programme, where they receive bespoke support in disengaging from extremist ideology (that is, cognitive change) and the intention to act in alignment with that ideology (that is, behavioural change) (HM Government 2012).

These programmes have come under increasing criticism by politicians and academics on the left for racially profiling ethnic communities and on the right for mainstreaming radical religious leaders. The strands of criticism do not necessarily contradict each other, as counter-terrorism programmes dealing with prevention of violent extremism have not always supported moderate voices but also those with questionable views on issues such as civil liberties, sexuality, and women's rights (Maher and Frampton 2009). Simultaneously, the majority of these projects have been designed for Muslim communities with potentially counter-productive effects. Criticism has emerged that Muslims have increasingly started distrusting the UK government, as they felt that it was not only targeting terrorists but also viewed their community through a security lens. A telling example of this is Project Champion in Birmingham, whereby West Midlands Police used counter-terrorism funds to install 218 video cameras in an area with a sizable Muslim population. After hefty criticism, the decision was taken to remove all 'spy' cameras (BBC News 2011).

BIG DATA: ISOLATING DRIVERS, TARGETING POTENTIAL TERRORISTS

With the exponential rise of available data in a digital age, it should come as no surprise that data is taking centre stage in the state's response. First of all, Big Data is also part of 'harder' counter-terrorism measures; emblematic for the War on Terror is the regular military action against (suspected) al Qaeda or Islamic State fighters in countries such as Iraq, Syria, Yemen, and Pakistan with Unmanned Aerial Vehicles (UAVs, or 'drones'). These drone attacks rely heavily on intercepting Signals Intelligence (Sigint) and geo-locating mobile phones of terrorists. When the green light is given, the phone is then targeted with a drone strike in the hope that the terrorist is killed. It is no surprise that the legality and legitimacy of this policy are disputed mainly due to the vast amount of unintended civilian casualties (Ackerman 2014). This chapter does not intend to deal with this pertinent question; instead, it explores how Big Data is becoming a key driver for the 'softer' Counter-Terrorism (CT), CVE, and de-radicalisation programmes.

Since the Edward Snowden revelations, the wider public has been introduced to the novel ways intelligence and security agencies rely on mass data sets for tracking potential terrorist networks and their activities. The algorithms employed are designed to monitor email and social media traffic, for instance, for specific key words and check for suspicious travel movements to countries such as Turkey (as a gateway to join al Qaeda or the Islamic State in Syria), Somalia, or Yemen. Financial transactions, which can reveal networks and the planning of operations, are also a growing source for intelligence. These and other bases of information are leading to a better-informed threat picture as well as prosecutions for CT-related offenses, such as plotting of terrorist attacks at home or joining a terrorist organisation abroad. Big Data becomes really interesting (or scary, depending on how you look at it) when individuals are deemed a future threat, as in cases referred to the UK's Channel programme in the absence of concrete evidence to prosecute individual X or Y at the moment but where the available evidence suggests someone is an elevated risk. Does it matter that this inference is done by a Big Data algorithm instead of a psychologist or social worker?

Big Data holds the—until now—unfulfilled promise to isolate drivers for terrorism and help us better understand the radicalisation process. If Big Data is about probability and correlation, then empowering large data sets, and understanding how to harvest their potential, may increase the understanding of what makes someone decide to commit a terrorist act. Until recently, the debates in the field of terrorism studies have yet to provide us with a concise range of drivers for terrorism. It could be argued that our understanding has been halted at the point of describing radicalisation at micro (the individual), meso (group-dynamics and networks), and macro levels (related to state policies and society at large) (Schmid 2013). Whilst this framework is useful in understanding the various levels of radicalisation and how they interlock, it facilitates descriptive research and struggles to explain the relationship between violent ideas and violent action. With the notion of radicalisation, it is implied that, for terrorists, action follows ideas; however, this causality is disputed (Ranstorp 2010; Schmid 2013). After years of studying radicalisation, academics and practitioners have yet to provide a thorough explanation of why certain extremists fail to act, whilst others with less extreme ideas have gone off to join terrorist organisations. The example of Yusuf Sarwar and Mohammed Ahmed springs to mind; they bought *Islam for Dummies* before heading off to Syria to join the jihad (Hasan 2014).

As governments and the private sector gather immense data sets, including data on virtually every citizen and consumer, practitioners and policy managers have a lot to gain by correlating the data of known terrorists. Information on, for instance, terrorists' socio-economic status, relationships, online behaviour, or even sleeping and eating patterns could build a tool-box that widens our understanding of the radicalisation process. Research by Gambetta and Hertog (2009) revealed that a significant proportion of Islamic extremists have an engineering degree, up to four times higher than expected. There may be dozens of other factors that are somehow connected to either extremism or terrorism. Big Data potentially holds the key to isolating these drivers, providing insight into how they relate to other drivers and providing cues on their place and time in the radicalisation process. These cues could become life-savers as they optimise the work of intelligence analysts and provide better models to signal radicalisation.

It is inevitable that the private sector and intelligence agencies start developing such 'smart' algorithms based on Big Data. The potential of customer and market segmentation techniques as successfully executed by the likes of Amazon, Google, and Walmart, combined with the elevated threat of terrorism and extremism in Europe, are strong drivers to ensure that such solutions will be developed. But it is vital that academics and subject matter experts be involved in this process, scrutinising its validity and providing a safeguard so that these techniques do not end up profiling migrant, religious, or ethnic communities. Moreover, Big Data should not just inform decision-making on security issues, but also be mobilised to help us to better understand radicalisation. If radicalisation and extremism are increasingly used to explain the threat of terrorism, then researchers need to be able to get access to as much data as ethically possible to understand these links. Big Data creates manifold opportunities for *understanding* terrorism, not merely *countering* it.

Beyond the debate on the appropriateness and legality of the use of bulk data, these algorithms are sometimes criticised for producing 'false positives'. This particular issue stems from the nature of the problem. Terrorism, luckily, is a relatively rare phenomenon for EU-member states: a high-impact, low-likelihood event. In 2011, *The Daily Telegraph* cited a government source who said that the UK faces approximately 200 potential terrorists living inside Britain (Rayment 2011). With the population over 60 million, the false positive paradox, whereby false positives are more frequently encountered than true positives, is bound to emerge. Therefore, even if an agency's state-of-the-art technique designed to identify potential terrorists is very accurate, it is highly likely to falsely implicate innocent citizens. This hazard can be reduced only by limiting the scope of the target population. This process, in turn, holds the risk of missing outliers—that is, certain lone wolves, such as the Norwegian far-right terrorist Anders Breivik. These examples highlight Big Data's tendency to focus on past events. For instance, travel to certain countries in which terrorist-related activities are assumed to take place can trigger a suspicious warning system. However, these countries have been selected based on travel movements by previous extremists. After the 2013 Boston bombing, for instance, algorithms might have been adjusted to give more weight to travel to Chechnya or Dagestan, even though it remains unclear if the Boston bombers' nationality, and/or visit to Dagestan, influenced their decision to carry out the attacks. Like other security planning and policies, algorithms can end up 'fighting the last war'.

The tools that governments employ today seek to identify whether suspected individuals have, or are in the process of absorbing, radical ideas and ideologies. Despite the vast range of technological developments and increased attention to terrorism in the West in recent times, intelligence agencies still often rely on Human Intelligence (Humint) to assess whether an individual merely has radical ideas or whether he or she will potentially turn these ideas into violent action. The decision, it could be argued, may be influenced by the intuition of intelligence agents instead of by more objective data. Big Data could change this decision-making process significantly and prioritise data over human intuition. It should be noted that data, in itself, is never objective. Relying solely on data to decide whether someone is a potential terrorist risks creating a dystopian future where false probabilities could destroy innocent lives; this possibility lies behind the science-fiction film 'Minority Report', in which murder is predicted before it occurs, but the prediction fails in one instance in which a police officer himself becomes the victim of a false accusation.

THE ROLE OF NON-STATE ACTORS

Western governments increasingly seek to work together with non-state actors in countering violent extremism. The reasoning for collaboration is relatively straight-forward: these actors hold access to data, which intelligence agencies need in order to paint a richer picture, on potential radicalising individuals or groups. A teacher might spot pupils getting interested in radical ideas or displaying extremist symbols; a general practitioner might sense a worrisome change in the mental state of patient; a local youth worker will likely pick up signals on the formation of networks in a local community. Pooling this data increases the likelihood of creating a better understanding of potential extremists.

How does Big Data fit in the inter-actor approach which is currently advocated by Western governments and specifically in EU counter-terrorism strategy? Currently, much data is gathered by state agencies that have direct or indirect contact with non-state actors. However, as information increasingly gets digitised and digitalised, it will be a lot easier for intelligence practitioners to harvest data from frontline contacts—the previously mentioned non-state actors—about potential extremists. This development could radically alter the relationship that the state builds with these frontline contacts, as all the state requires is that they hand over valuable data. Increasing digitalisation reduces the need for personal contacts, and, thus, effectively alters the relationship between the state and non-state actors and between frontline workers in the communities and the (back-office) intelligence agencies.

The current relationship is grounded in creating non-hierarchical, horizontal security networks in which all parties share information for the common good. The question is how this relationship will take shape in a Big Data age, when the decision-making model could change and the equality of these networks is under threat by a more powerful state. How will the various non-governmental actors cope with their new role, and could this interaction produce a civil rebellion against too much power wielded by the state and its security apparatus? Substantial criticism has already emerged in the UK on the introduction of the Counter Terrorism and Security Act of 2015, which forces schools and universities to report signals of extremism to the authorities (Sky News 2015). The state essentially walks a tightrope in this type of policing, as it risks not only alienating certain communities from the state, but driving them away from schools, universities and civil society.

THE PRIVATE SECTOR AND ONLINE RADICALISATION

Beyond the first-line contacts, the role of Internet Service Providers (ISPs) and internet giants such as Google, Facebook, and Twitter is pivotal in countering extremism, as the internet has become the foremost domain where radical ideologies are shared between like-minded individuals. Both the ISPs and online service providers gather vast amounts of data on virtually everyone, which governments can then tap into to monitor potentially violent individuals and networks. From jihadists to extreme-right groups to animal right activists, all are united by '(1) a potential to use violence and (2) the usage of the internet and social media to share their ideology, recruit new members, and discuss plans for actions. Therefore, European governments are increasingly aware that they have to fight these groups not just in 'the real world', but also online.

EU governments rely on two strategies to wage this online battle. First, they pursue efforts to outlaw and delete extremist content on the internet. A prime example of this is the online magazine 'Inspire', produced by Al Qaeda in the Arabian Peninsula (AQAP) and designed to incite Western Muslims to wage jihad. The English-language glossy provides practical tips to its supporters on how to execute terrorist attacks and kill as many 'infidels' as possible. Many European governments have decided to force ISPs to delete the publication from their servers. This strategy has proven largely unsuccessful, as the magazine has kept reappearing, like a game of whack-a-mole, on other servers and websites. The British government has even gone so far as prosecuting its readers: a Muslim woman was sentenced to a year in prison for having downloaded two editions on her mobile phone in 2012 (The Guardian 2012). It should be noted that this repressive strategy, focused on banning unwanted content on the internet, is criticised for being counter-productive and practically near-impossible to execute, as digital information tends to emerge elsewhere (Stevens and Neumann 2009).

A second strategy to deal with extremist content online is the dissemination of credible counter narratives that de-legitimise terrorism in general and jihad in particular. The rationale for this approach is that, while banning extremist content will make it only more attractive, de-glorifying terrorism will be more successful in countering radicalisation and will ultimately mitigate the risk of further radicalisation. In this strategy, governments engage with NGOs and so-called 'moderate voices' to empower and disseminate their messages. Evaluation of these programmes, however, is lacking, as it is hard to measure the impact of moderate voices related to de-radicalisation. Perhaps Big Data will offer insight into this approach, as governments are better equipped through digitalisation of online contact to track progress and the influence of outsiders in this process.

Governments could also learn from the usage of Big Data in the advertising industry. As discussed earlier, multinationals seek access to vast data sets of (potential) consumers. Advertising, consequently, is becoming increasingly targeted at the individual and his or her deeply personal interests. The algorithms used by the digital giants could very well provide governments with a model to approach vulnerable individuals with timely positive messages that de-glorify and de-legitimise extremist ideas and actions. If Big Data does indeed offer insight into the stages or timeline of the radicalisation process, government could use this advantage to target individuals based on their current stage of radicalisation.

Before one can design such a strategy, access to online personal data is required; Google, Facebook, ISPs, and governments must share collected data so as to have ways to access this source that meet with thresholds of public consent and widely shared views on appropriate ethical behaviour. The PRISM revelations have shed light on the magnitude of these operations undertaken by the National Security Agency (NSA) and the Government Communications Headquarters (GCHQ). In addition, Facebook has started revealing statistics on governments' request for access to users' information, such as private pictures and conversations (Lee 2013).

It should be noted that Big Data in itself does not create successful de-radicalisation strategies. It is merely a tool that could produce probabilities of the drivers and stages of the radicalisation process. Human agency will likely continue to be required to contextualise the information, make sense of individual cases, and remove false positives. Therefore, it will be highly unlikely that algorithms will totally replace Humint in the near future. However, aggregating data from a variety of sources to build a richer intelligence picture is increasingly becoming the *modus operandi*.

CONCLUSIONS

The Big Data revolution will undoubtedly produce new insights into the drivers of (de)radicalisation and shed light on the stages of the process. These effects should enable governments to detect potential terrorists in a timely way and help optimise counter-terrorism strategies, but also help us better understand the relationship between extremist ideas and extremist behaviour (that is, terrorism). As Big Data and algorithms will likely take centre stage in this process, academics and subject matter experts need to be closely involved to study the inferences based on data. Academia has a role in scrutinising Big Data intelligence in order to prevent negative consequences and public blowback related to algorithmic practices. In exchange, the intelligence community and its partners could share their data in a safe and secure way to help academics better understand the radicalisation process and the link between extremism and terrorism.

Increased probabilities of violent extremism, however, will never fully stop all forms of terrorism, and democratic governments will need to continue engaging disenfranchised citizens in order to prevent them from committing political violence. Big Data does not take away the need to write and employ counter-narratives that de-glorify and de-legitimise terrorist acts.

REFERENCES

BBC News. (2011). Birmingham Project Champion 'spy' cameras being removed. Retrieved from http://www.bbc.co.uk/news/uk-england-birmingham-13331161

Council of the European Union. (2005a, November 24). The European Union strategy for combating radicalisation and recruitment to terrorism. Retrieved from http://register.consilium.europa.eu/pdf/en/05/st14/st14781-re01.en05.pdf

Council of the European Union. (2005b, November 30). The European Union-terrorism strategy. Retrieved from http://register.consilium.eu.int/pdf/en/05/st14/st14469-re04.en05.pdf

Gambetta, D., & Hertog, S. (2009). Why are there so many engineers among Islamic radicals? *Archives Européennes de Sociologie, 50*(2), 201–230.

Hasan, M. (2014). What the Jihadists who bought 'Islam for Dummies' on Amazon tell us about radicalisation. *Huffington Post*. Retrieved from http://www.huffingtonpost.co.uk/mehdi-hasan/jihadist-radicalisation-islam-for-dummies_b_5697160.html

HM Government. (2011, July). CONTEST: The United Kingdom's strategy for countering terrorism. Retrieved from https://www.gov.uk/government/uploads/system/uploads/attachment_data/file/97994/contest-summary.pdf

HM Government. (2012, October). Channel: Protecting vulnerable people from being drawn into terrorism. A guide for local partnerships. Retrieved from http://www.npcc.police.uk/documents/TAM/2012/201210TAMChannel Guidance.pdf

HM Government. (2015, October). Counter-extremism strategy. Retrieved from https://www.gov.uk/government/uploads/system/uploads/attachment_data/file/470088/51859_Cm9148_Accessible.pdf

Lee, D. (2013, August 27). Government requests to Facebook outlined in report. *BBC News*. Retrieved from http://www.bbc.co.uk/news/technology-23852230

Maher, S., & Frampton, M. (2009, March 8). Choosing our friends wisely: Criteria for engagement with Muslim groups. *Policy Exchange*. Retrieved from http://www.policyexchange.org.uk/publications/category/item/choosing-our-friends-wisely-criteria-for-engagement-with-muslim-groups

Ranstorp, M. (2010). Introduction. In M. Ranstorp (Ed.), *Understanding violent radicalisation: Terrorist and jihadist movements in Europe*. New York: Routledge.

Rayment, S. (2011, October 8). 200 suicide bombers 'planning attacks in UK'. *The Telegraph*. Retrieved from http://www.telegraph.co.uk/news/uknews/terrorism-in-the-uk/8815574/200-suicide-bombers-planning-attacks-in-UK.html

Schmid, A. (2013). *Radicalisation, de-radicalisation, counter-radicalisation: A conceptual discussion and literature review*. ICCT Research Paper. Retrieved from http://www.icct.nl/download/file/ICCT-Schmid-Radicalisation-De-Radicalisation-Counter-Radicalisation-March-2013_2.pdf

Sky News. (2015, July 1). Anti-radicalisation law introduced in UK. Retrieved from http://news.sky.com/story/1511229/anti-radicalisation-law-introduced-in-uk

Stevens, T., & Neumann, P. (2009). Countering online radicalisation: A strategy for action. *The International Centre for the Study of Radicalisation and Political Violence*. Retrieved from http://icsr.info/wp-content/uploads/2012/10/12 36768491ICSROnlineRadicalisationReport.pdf

The Guardian. (2012, December 6). Woman jailed after al-Qaida terrorist material found on her phone. *The Guardian*. Retrieved from http://www.theguardian.com/world/2012/dec/06/woman-jailed-al-qaida-material-on-phone

CHAPTER 9

Enhancing Intelligence-Led Policing: Law Enforcement's Big Data Revolution

Ian Stanier

Abstract This chapter offers an overview of primary Big Data sets 'owned' by or formally accessible to UK law enforcement. It examines, through the lens of practitioners, how Big Data is utilised in mitigating identified or anticipated harm to individuals and communities. It outlines accompanying oversight and governance arrangements. The chapter explores key organisational, technological, ethical, and cultural challenges faced by law enforcement seeking to exploit Big Data when discharging legal responsibilities in safeguarding communities, reducing crime, and addressing anti-social behaviour. This chapter concludes that Big Data is critical for enhanced public safety but that optimal use is hampered by inadequate staff skills, technological dysfunctionality, organisational risk aversion to information, and an absence of engagement and effort with the public.

Keywords Big Data • Intelligence-led policing • Data management • Law enforcement • Oversight bodies • Intelligence gathering • Intelligence agencies • Policing

I. Stanier (✉)
Associate Lecturer, University of Portsmouth,
Institute of Criminal Justice Studies, Portsmouth, UK

© The Editor(s) (if applicable) and The Author(s) 2016   97
A. Bunnik et al. (eds.), *Big Data Challenges*,
DOI 10.1057/978-1-349-94885-7_9

INTRODUCTION

Law enforcement organisations routinely secure intelligence from varied overt, discrete, and covert sources. Advances in technology, in society, and the economy and the proliferation of Big Data have driven this collection activity into uncharted territory. Whilst acknowledging the volumes of data flowing from an extraordinarily deep and wide open-source well (Olesker 2012), including social media (HMIC 2011; Omand et al. 2012; Bartlett et al. 2013), the core of this chapter is focused on nine critical Big Data closed systems governed and routinely used by all UK law enforcement organisations.

Other Big Data systems exist in the UK, such as the National Special Branch Intelligence System (NSBIS),[1] which now includes the National Domestic Extremism Database, the National Ballistics Intelligence Service (NABIS) database, and Pentip (penalty notices). However, these systems are restricted to specific departments or are not, in the case of PentiP and NABIS datasets, routinely used by the majority of policing professionals. The selection of the nine critical systems is primarily based on their routine access by police officers and staff.

Nor does Big Data include those national systems owned by criminal justice partners. It omits Her Majesty's Prison Service's Mercury intelligence system and its Computer-National Offender Management Information System (C-NOMIS), the National Crime Agency's managed Violence and Sex Offender Register (ViSOR), or the Driver Vehicle Licensing Agency (DVLA) database.[2] Many of these systems offer direct access to law enforcement staff undertaking specialist functions or indirect access under other legislation or memoranda of understanding. Nor does this chapter cover commercially available data sets accessed by law enforcement, through payment or otherwise (communication companies or financial companies including Experian, the Insurance Fraud Bureau, or GB Accelerator).

THE 'BIG NINE'; LAW ENFORCEMENT BIG DATA SYSTEMS

The nine Big Data systems are the Emergency Services Network (ESN), the e-Borders programme, the Holmes2 investigation system, National ANPR Datacentre (NADC), the National Fingerprint and Biometrics Database IDENT1, the National DNA Database (NDNAD), the Police National Computer (PNC), the Police National Database (PND), and the

Schengen Information System (SISII). Whilst these systems are not silver bullets for solving crime, their use of Big Data provides deep insight into criminal behaviour and emerging risks. All improve law enforcement's understanding of community needs, enhance operational agility and timeliness in targeting the right offenders, and promote the discovery of new threats to communities. As the chapter unfolds, it addresses challenges in the systems' use and development and introduces the oversight bodies that monitor collection, use, and management of the product. Finally, it will bring in the public debate about privacy and law enforcement's use of Big Data.

The Emergency Services Network (ESN) provides integrated voice and broadband data service for the UK emergency services (police, fire and rescue, and ambulance) and 300 other organisations. It generates geolocation information, deployment timings, and command and control information, all vital in understanding efficiencies and effectiveness of a multi-billion-pound public sector. Effective analysis of its data can ensure the right officers are in the right location at the right time and undertake the right response.

E-borders, launched in 2003, is an Advanced Passenger Information (API) system that tracks approximately 80% of airline passengers and crew in and out of the United Kingdom. The Big Data generated includes travel document information (TDI) and service information, passenger name and address details, telephone numbers, travel itinerary and ticketing information, airline details, and departure and arrival points. The data is shared between law enforcement and the Home Office and is cross-referenced against terrorist and criminal watch lists, including wanted and missing-persons information. Checks are undertaken using the Remote Semaphore National Border Tracking Centre (NBTC) platform.

The Home Office Large Major Enquiry System (HOMLES2) is used by, and links with, all forces for major incident investigations, including murder and serious and complex crime. It supports missing-person enquiries and operational disaster requirements, including the management of mass casuality incidents and large-scale evacuations.

There are two key biometrics Big Data sets. The first is IDENT1, the replacement for the National Automated Fingerprint identification System (NAFIS), which serves as the central national service in the UK for storing, searching, and comparing biometric information on those arrested and detained by police. It is interoperable with other fingerprint technology such as Livescan, which electronically scans the fingerprints of a person in custody. It holds fingerprints of 7.1 million people who have encountered the criminal justice system and annually verifies over 1.5 million arrested detainees. The second is the National DNA Database (NDNAD), which, since 2013, has generated more than 446,000 matches to crimes (Home Office 2013, p. 5). It holds both an individual's DNA and samples taken from crime scenes and, in 2013, held 6,737,973 DNA profiles from individuals and 428,634 crime scene DNA profiles, such as DNA found at burglaries or murder scenes (Home Office 2013, p. 5).[3]

The National Automatic Number Plate Recognition (ANPR) Datacentre (NADC) is central to the monitoring of offenders using the road network. ANPR technology is used to read vehicle number plates and cross-references them against other datasets. The number-plate reading devices (NRD) can be vehicle-mounted, static, or moveable, and can view multi-road lanes. They are CCTV-integrated or hand-held, and are generally linked to a Back Office Function (BOF) which allows it to run the vehicle number plates against large data sets, including the Police National Computer (PNC), the Driver and Vehicle Licensing Agency (DVLA), and the Motor Insurance Database (MIDAS).

Investigators can search for matching data through the National ANPR datacentre (NADC), which records the plate's location, the time it was read, and the image captured. The effectiveness of ANPR Big Data is best when analysed in the context of other sources of information (CCTV, financial information, stop and search, and intelligence). It supports both reactive (locating stolen vehicles, identification of movement of a vehicle during the commission of a crime, researching alibis, and identifying potential suspects, victims, and witnesses) and proactive operations (locating a vehicle in support of a surveillance operation, initiating an arrest to prevent crime, reducing disorder, and researching the movements of offenders to identify lifestyle patterns and predict future offending locations).

The ANPR systems capture and record imagery. After ANPR reads a number plate and cross-references it against a law enforcement database, an alert alarm will be generated within six seconds to inform a decision for deployment. These alerts are triggered by markers used by the PNC such as 'Firearms', 'Suicidal', 'Sex Offender', and 'Drugs'.

Law enforcement's use of imagery capture is underpinned by the National ANPR Standards for Policing document, drafted to reflect the Surveillance Camera Codes of Practice issued under the provisions of the Protection of Freedom Act of 2012. An awareness of the increasingly transnational nature of organised crime means that the standards now include a commitment to ensuring that systems are capable of reading plates from all members of the Schengen community. Necessity and justification for NRD deployments must now be based on known locations critical in detecting, deterring, and disrupting criminality. This practice means an intelligence basis is found within analytical base products, such as strategic assessments or a problem profile. Where the pressing need cannot be evidenced, the Information Commissioner's office (ICO) can issue an enforcement notice to require a force to review its ANPR deployments.[4]

The Police National Computer (PNC), launched in 1975, was the first Big Data law enforcement system. Accessible to all UK police forces and law enforcement agencies, it holds personal descriptions, bail conditions, court convictions, custodial history, warning markers, wanted or missing reports, and pending prosecutions records. It also holds records, including number plate registrations, make, colour, register keeper details, DVLA markers, police reports, and vehicle insurance details, of all vehicles in the UK (Home Office 2014a). It is used on a daily basis by frontline officers undertaking routine policing, including stop-and-searches of people and vehicles.[5] Investigators and intelligence officers utilise its research functionality, including QUEST (Querying using Enhanced or Extended Search Techniques), which searches partial known characteristics of people and VODS (Vehicle Online Descriptive Search) for vehicle-related investigations.

The Police National Database (PND) is arguably one of the largest and most important UK law enforcement Big Data systems, whose purpose, according to the College of Policing, is 'to support the achievement of three strategic benefits which are: to safeguard children and vulnerable people, counter-terrorism, and prevent and disrupt crime'.[6] Born out of information management and sharing failures arising from the tragic 2004 Soham murders of two children at the hands of a suspected sex offender (Bichard 2004), it now holds over 2.9 billion law enforcement records, a figure swelled by the daily updates of forces' and agencies' copies of all police records of intelligence, custody, crime, and domestic and child abuse investigations. It is underpinned by the Code of Practice on the operation and use of the Police National Database made by the Home Secretary in 2010, under section 39A, Police Act 1996.

Schengen Information System (SISII) is a pan-European database generating 45 million alerts (European Commission 2015) concerning people and property in participating countries. It supports external border control and law enforcement cooperation in the Schengen states, with its main purpose 'to help preserve internal security in the Schengen States in the absence of internal border checks' (European Commission 2015). The SISII database is underpinned by three legal instruments relating to border control cooperation (Regulation (EC) No. 1987/2006), law enforcement cooperation (Council Decision 2007/533/JHA), and cooperation on vehicle registration (Regulation (EC) No. 1986/2006).

Access to the data is through the Central Schengen Information System (C.SIS) via a country's National Schengen Information System (N.SISII). Each country will manage alerts through its own Supplementary Information Request at the National Entry (SIRENE) Bureau. The SIRENE Bureau will be allied to other international law enforcement areas, including EUROPOL and INTERPOL.

The SISII alerts include those for persons wanted for arrest for extradition (Article 26), alerts for missing persons who need police protection or a place of safety (Article 32),[7] alerts for witnesses or for absconders or subjects of criminal judgements to appear before judicial authorities (Article 34), alerts relating to people or vehicles requiring discreet checks (Article 36), and alerts for objects that are misappropriated, lost, stolen, or evidence and are sought for the purposes of seizure (Article 38).

OVERSIGHT AND BIG DATA

Whilst some of the UK's oversight bodies have overlapping functions and differing statutory footings, all are focused on ensuring legislative compliance, protecting the public's interests, and the investigation and resolution of complaints. All the law enforcement systems fall under one or more oversight bodies subject to the functionality performed by the data access and its subsequent use (Fig. 9.1).

A second layer of oversight is delivered by Her Majesty's Inspectorate of Constabulary (HMIC), a body with a statutory responsibility to inspect police forces in England and Wales and assess activity across a wide-ranging spectrum of policing activity, including use information, ICT, and Big-Data-related issues (HMIC 2013, 2014a, 2015a, 2015b, 2015c, 2015d).

Oversight Body	Area of responsibility
Information Commissioners Office (ICO)	Responsible for upholding information rights[1] under *Data Protection Act 1998* (DPA), the *Freedom of Information Act 2000* (FOIA), the *Environmental Information Regulations 2004* (EIRs) and the *Protection of Freedoms Act 2012* (PoFA).
Interception of Communications Commissioner's Office (IOCCO)	Reviews compliance with *Regulation of Investigatory Powers Act 2000* powers associated with interception, acquisition and disclosure of communication. Additionally is monitors Prison Act 1952 interception.
Office of the Biometrics Commissioner	Reviews the retention and use by police of DNA samples, DNA profiles and fingerprints.
Office of Surveillance Commissioners (OSC)	Monitors compliance with the covert policing powers under the *Regulation of Investigatory Powers Act 2000* and Part III of the *Police Act 1997*
Surveillance Camera Commissioner	Ensures compliance with the use of cameras and the Surveillance Codes of Practice

Fig. 9.1   Oversight bodies relevant to Big Data and UK law enforcement
[1]https://ico.org.uk (accessed 17/05/2015)

FUTURE CHALLENGES FOR LAW ENFORCEMENT AND THE USE OF BIG DATA

Progress in the development and management of Big Data by law enforcement is self-evident, but considerable challenges remain. These challenges primarily fall into five key areas. The first relates to reviewing legislative frameworks and associated practices. The second centres on the requirement for smart information and application architecture that integrates and enables law enforcement service delivery. The third area requires a radical transformation and mainstreaming of staff capability to manage and exploit Big Data. The fourth requires a fundamental shift in existing collaborative connections with the private sector and other non-traditional actors. Finally, the fifth challenge area focuses on law enforcement's relationship with the diverse range of social groups it serves in the context of interference with privacy.

Associated legislation and practice risk being outdated, and, in some cases, unlawful or legally ambiguous. Public trust and consent, the very bedrock of policing legitimacy, are vulnerable, as more data is collected against a narrative of escalating privacy concerns. However, the law must remain protean and responsive to contemporary policing issues. This legislative and process review must be undertaken against a background of economic truths. Whilst Big Data and analytical techniques offer the possibility of releasing law enforcement staff to focus on priority areas or operational activity required technology-related procurements are at odds with the new reality of austerity-era budgets[8] (Home Office 2014). Complex legislation, over-cautious collection, and Big Data security arrangements still undermine technological opportunities by deterring user access.

Optimising Big Data value from these systems requires cutting-edge technologies docking with other existing data sets to enable rapid processing and analysis (and, in the case of crimes in action or threats to life, real-time processing). Linked to this process is the need for the findings to be effectively communicated in an accessible and a creatively visual format to potential users.

The operational benefits of this high-volume data require advanced analytical techniques and skilled interpretation. Consequently, the data can inform decision-making about the appropriate course of operational activity and response. However, the capabilities of law enforcement to routinely undertake this work effectively are in doubt and subject to criticism (HMIC 2015c, p. 42).

With advances in machine learning, simulation, and data mining, insight can be extracted from Big Data sets too complex, unstructured, and large for traditional analytical techniques. The advancement in Big Data technologies and applications outpaces the sector's user skills. Important delivery outcomes of the national policing curriculum are falling short and, as a consequence, law enforcement is ill-prepared to exploit the opportunities to reduce threat and harm that effective use of Big Data offers. Securing insight from Big Data will need more than technology, though. It will require highly trained professional data scientists who, in turn, must possess deep analytical skill sets. Training for intelligence officers is still inadequate (Stanier 2013), rarely lasting more than five days, with Big Data content negligible. The HMIC has identified an absence of force skills in new crime-related technology, with its inspection revealing that only 2 % of police staff across 37 forces have been trained in investigating cybercrime (HMIC 2014b, p. 14). Whilst some collaborative efforts to address the skills gaps have been launched, further effort is required to identify, recruit, develop, and retain talent.[9] This skill shortage is a problem across all sectors (House of Commons Science and Technology Committee 2014, p. 13). How law enforcement engages in this cross-sector *war for talent* will determine how it can successfully extract the operational value from its data.

Traditional analytical methods reach a quick stop when attempting to incorporate Big Data. Without processes ensuring that smart extraction secures only the required data (cleansed of inaccuracies and corrupted data and in a structured form), interpretation is difficult. Once satisfied with the quality of the Big Data, humans and computers must interact to allow contextual understanding, situational awareness, identification of biases, and anomalies within the data. Where the intention is to communicate the findings more widely to key stakeholders and decision-makers, consideration of how this communication is best achieved, for example in the use of visualisation software, needs to be explored.

Nonetheless, disproportionately high security arrangements have an impact on the extent of Big Data exploitation. Monthly audits reveal access by the licensed and trained operator PND Big Data was as low as 19% in one metropolitan force, and, nationally, monthly usage is just over 30%. Contributing to this failure to access are risk-averse security measures, including physical access requirements, and policies framed against low organisational acceptance of risk around information management. As a consequence, information collected by law enforcement in the course of its criminal justice activity lies dormant, its storage and retrieval systems passive, until some form of incident initiates search and access. Potentially important insights into crime prevention, detection, and reduction are not being realised. The value of the information it holds is left locked, but rising media and public expectations are now challenging law enforcement's capability and willingness to exploit Big Data. 'Citizen expectations are rising around crime reporting, emergency response effectiveness, citizen care, public safety and public involvement in policing' (Accenture 2013, p. 3). 'New' priority crimes of child sexual exploitation, modern-day slavery, and cyber-related offenses are complex in nature, with offenders operating across force boundaries and virtual worlds. All demand effective use of Big Data.

A contrasting access issue also manifests itself. A nationally-backed project introducing the Police National Database into English prisons on behalf of the National Offender Management Service (NOMS) stalled because the NOMS security group, fearful that the project would lead to an increase in identified risks to which they were duty-bound to respond, turned down the opportunity. This failure reinforces the challenges for law enforcement when it attempts to work collaboratively with risk-averse partners.

Whilst the focus of the chapter has been on law-enforcement owned or controlled Big Data sets, the commercialisation of private information (open to everyone, by payment or otherwise) introduces other ethical policing dilemmas. Intelligence collection is no longer dependent on police-collected data sets, but is informed through partnership data, mainly from public authorities but increasingly from private sector and non-governmental agencies. Policing increasingly involves knowledge that brokers among groups, organisations, and information intermediaries, including Google, ISP, Apple, and financial institutions (College of Policing 2015, p. 60). Whilst independent oversight and regulation is 'relatively' clear in terms of public authorities, it is less so in the private sector, with regulation sometimes voluntary and, on occasions, absent. How law enforcement proceeds with the capture and use of Big Data from these data brokers is still relatively unnavigated, yet, increasingly, austerity demands may see intelligence collection and analysis outsourced to the private sector. Outsourcing will be an issue not only for law enforcement but also for the oversight organisations.

Big Data costs are significant. The e-borders programme cost nearly half a billion pounds (Independent Chief Inspector of Borders and Immigration 2013), the Police National Database cost £75 million to develop (Information Age 2011), the national DNA Database costs over £1.4 million a year (Home Office 2013, p. 18), and, since its initiation, the Schengen SISII project cost nearly £120 million (European Commission 2013). The data revolution points to an expensive future for law enforcement. The outlay required for Big Data exploitation opens the possibility of the emergence of differing capabilities in smaller or poorer law enforcement agencies, leading to a Big Data 'first class and economy class'. Those that cannot afford investment may miss opportunities, including greater use of geospatial alerts for directing and informing patrolling officers; the use of augmented reality technologies that bring visual information directly to officers deployed at a scene; the use of drone feeds to simultaneously access Big Data sets to provide visual context and situational awareness; the possibilities of wearable Big Data capture technologies, including the use of 'heads-up displays' (HUD) providing live-time information to a serious unfolding incident based on an officer's emergency request or to the drawing of a Taser or firearm; and, finally, the use of Haptic Rings to deliver alerts to officers as they enter a hotspot, an area of concern for officer safety or as a prompt to collect intelligence in support of a task.

Access to Big Data systems can be both a blessing and a curse. Big Data results are not infallible. Some warn against an acceptance of such:

> Too often, Big Data enables the practice of apophenia: seeing patterns where none actually exist, simply because enormous quantities of data can offer connections that radiate in all directions. (Boyd and Crawford 2012, p. 11)

Dealing with such high volumes of data it is not only hard and complex, but also brings with it a risk of information overload, a perennial information-sharing pathology (Sheptycki 2004; Stanier 2013). Even with effective filtering, blending, and organisation of data, the practitioner can still be left with a mass of data requiring action. This overload can be seen in the experience of the National Border Targeting Centre, who, overseeing the e-border programme, deleted, in a ten month period, over 649,000 records relating to potential tobacco and drug smuggling without their being read (Independent Chief Inspector of Borders and Immigration 2013, p. 2). In one force area, the ANPR systems generated over 30,000 alerts from 900,000 daily number plate reads. With the exception of a crime in action, threat to life, or serious organised crime, nearly all ANPR alerts are ignored due to a lack of deployable resources (Stanier 2013, p. 163). There are not only exponential data volumes to which law enforcement has access, but also increasing demands for its interrogation by associated bodies, such as the Home-Office-funded Disclosure and Barring Service (DBS) (Hickey 2015). Requirements to cross-reference high volumes of data against other data sets, unless automated, are posing increasing challenges to users of information (Weinfass 2015). Without effectively processing and accessing this information, law enforcement is vulnerable to accusations of indiscriminate, disproportionate, and unnecessary data collection.

Optimising successful outcomes from interrogation of the nine Big Data systems is dependent on law enforcement utilising all of its relevant data sets. All source assessment is undermined by legacy systems operating in silos or unable to deliver inter- and intra- connectivity, a technical dysfunctionality undermining effectiveness in tackling serious and organised crime (HMIC 2015b; 2014c, p. 16). Furthermore, 'big' is not necessarily 'beautiful'. There will still be value in 'small' databases, whose information may be vitally important, nuanced, and rich with insightful data.

Society expects and understands the necessity for the police use of Big Data to defend against criminality. Yet, society is also critical of this use as part of a form of Orwellian state control. Amendments driven by *S and*

Marper (European Court of Human Rights App No. 30562/04)[10] and the provisions of the Protection of Freedoms Act 2012 have led to the removal of the majority of innocent parties from fingerprint and DNA databases. Legislative clarity is still required over the lawfulness of Big Data, including innocent parties' details and incorporating images held as part of the Police National Database's facial recognition functionality. Law enforcement has listened and reacted to public concerns, including the removal of large CCTV and ANPR infrastructures from socially sensitive areas,[11] and has addressed issues resulting from inquiry into poor police management of information (HMIC 2013, 2015d). Counter-intuitively, though, effective analytical interrogation of Big Data may reduce the risk of collateral intrusion into peoples' lives by the state. E-borders passenger information may direct police activity at an individual rather than intruding on the private lives of all the other passengers. 'Stop and search' may become increasingly targeted, reducing unnecessary intrusive police-public contacts. Nonetheless, these decisions need to be part of a meaningful and informed engagement with the public.

Conclusions

Law enforcement is institutionally wired to collect data. The police are, and have always been, 'information workers'. Haggerty observed that '[i]ndeed, the police are remarkably enthusiastic collectors of information, displaying a desire to amass and secure access to volumes of data that far surpass their ability to make it pragmatically useful' (Haggerty 2012, p. 235). Big Data, open data, and data infrastructures are yet to be fully understood in terms of digital policing and the possibilities of opportunities arising from new data analytics. Big Data may open the possibility of reliable predictive analysis. It would, however, be entirely consistent, but mistaken, to dismiss public concerns that include caution even on viewing Big Data:

> The data revolution poses a number of thorny questions with respect to the extent to which everyday lives are being captured in data assemblages and how people's data body precedes and conditions their lives in all kinds of unanticipated ways. (Kitchin 2014, p. 187)

The counter-narrative warns against an over-cautious and extreme privacy-rights approach. Some have argued that 'the common good is being systematically neglected out of excessive deference to privacy' (Etzioni 1999, p. 4) and that liberty and security must be balanced with public safety requirements (Posner 2006). Big Data must be mined with the consent of communities, on behalf of communities, and in support of communities. Doing so is, however, an on-going effort. Cultural attitudes, behaviours, and norms continually shift. Communities are not homogenous constructs[12] (European Commission 2011, p. 324) and social demographics also come into consideration (European Commission 2011, p. 205).[13] Policy and practice associated with Big Data, where possible, need to reflect these issues. Public support may depend on specific use of the data for perceived personal and social benefits. Surveys reveal public support for the use of data as part of an effort in crime prevention and detection and the discovery of fraud and dishonest behaviour (Sciencewise Expert Resource Centre 2014, p. 1). Other surveys reveal significant support for police and UK intelligence agencies to access their data in investigations of minor crimes (61%), serious crimes (86%) and terrorism or threats to life situations (88%) where a person is a suspect (Ipsos MORI 2014). Whilst support is substantial, law enforcement must not be complacent, should be open, and should maintain an ongoing discourse with the public in a changing data and policing landscape. Police forces have a responsibility to ensure that the public voice is heard amongst the volume of operational vested interests.

Lessons from earlier inquiries (Bichard 2004) must be learnt. The concept of 'critical intelligence loss', where important data held by law enforcement is not shared or accessed when required and as a consequence, undermines an investigation or an operational response. In practical terms, law enforcement cannot not know what it knows:

> The oxygen of effective policing is information, but it is useless if it cannot be found and used at the same time and in the circumstances in which it is needed. And in policing, if it is inaccessible to those who need it, great harm may occur which could and should have been prevented. (HMIC 2014c, p. 16)

If we have information or access to information that informs the selection of the most effective and proportionate operational response to identified harm, then there is a moral organisational *and* public duty to secure, store, manage, and utilise that data accordingly. This point was reinforced by the HMIC:

Seemingly one-off instances of suspicious or criminal behaviour assume a greater importance if it can be shown, by linking information, that they are not isolated, but form a pattern of behaviour that gives rise to concern. (HMIC 2015d, p. 8)

Information is the lifeblood of law enforcement and the nine critical Big Data systems, properly utilised and integrated with other platforms, can produce better services, serve as effective operational tools, save lives, and reduce harm to individuals and communities. Nonetheless, just because law enforcement can utilise Big Data does not mean that it should. There are differential and contrary consequences to its misuse. How successful law enforcement is in its use of Big Data will not only be determined by its utilisation by the Front Line to protect people, but also to the extent that its use receives prior and informed public consent.

NOTES

1. The NSBIS system is soon to be replaced by a *National Common Intelligence Platform* (NCIA) as part of the ACPO TAM funded APPOLLO programme.
2. The DVLA database holds all licensed and unlicensed vehicles registered in GB and included 80 million records including vehicle number plates http://data.gov.uk/dataset/dvla-vehicles-database (Accessed 01/07/2015).
3. This figure reflected a fall from 7,178,359 profiles held in 2012 when innocent DNA profiles were also retained. The *Protection of Freedoms Act* 2012 has led to most innocent peoples DNA profiles and fingerprints removed and destroyed.
4. In July 2013, the ICO issued an Enforcement notice against Hertfordshire Constabulary for their use of ANPR cameras around the town of Royston which captured the movement of any vehicles entering or leaving the town. The ICO was unconvinced that adequate impact assessments had been prepared prior to their introduction. http://ico.org.uk/action_weve_taken/Enforcement/hertfordshire-constabulary/ [Accessed 28/06/2015].
5. The *National Policing Improvement Agency* (NPIA) revealed in 2009 that the PNC held 9.2 million nominal records, 52 million driver records, 55 million vehicle records and that 185 million transactions were made in 2008 alone (Source: NPIA Business Plan 2009–2012, p. 32) A *Freedom of information Act* request revealed the figure for nominal records had increased to 11,547,847 as of 17/10/2014 https://www.gov.uk/government/publications/nominal-criminal-records-on-the-police-national-computer [Accessed 28/06/2015].

6. College of Policing *'PND Police National Database'* www.college.police. uk/What-we-do/Learning/Curriculum/ICT/PND_National_Database/ pages/default.aspx (Accessed 20/05/2015).

7. A recent success concerned the stopping of a 16 year-old girl at the Hungarian-Romanian border en route to Syria due to the SISII alert. She was detained in a place of safety and returned to the Netherlands.

8. Police budgets in England and Wales have seen a 20% reduction since 2011 (Source BBC *'Police forces all face major budget cuts'* 07/03/2015 www. bbc.co.uk/news/uk-31771456 [Accessed 05/05/2015]). Police Officers now stand at 127,909, their lowest number since 2002. Support staff, Police Community Support Officers, police staff and designated officers have all seen reduction in numbers over the last 12 months. Home Office Police Workforce Numbers, England and Wales, 31 March 2014 http://www.gov. uk/government/publications/police-workforce-england-and-wales-31-march-2014/police-workforce-england-and-wales-31-march-2014 [Accessed 09/05/2015].

9. The National Business Area for Intelligence's *Intelligence Innovation Group* and Liverpool Hope University have collaborated to design and offer an *Executive MA Intelligence, Analytics and Media.*

10. The *S and Marper v UK* (2008) *App No. 30562/04* ruling held that the indefinite retention of DNA samples and profiles taken from innocent people is a violation of Article 8 of the ECHR.

11. The *Project Champion Review (2010)* inquired into the West Midlands Police's plan to install a network of 169 ANPR cameras, provided by the Terrorism and Allied Matters fund, around the Sparkbrook and Washwood Heath areas of Birmingham. The cameras were subsequently decommissioned and removed after community opposition.

12. European attitudes also significantly vary. Response to the question *'The police sometimes access and analyse individuals' personal data to carry out their activities. In what circumstances should the police be* able *to access individuals' personal data?* Estonians reported the lowest support (17%) to provide access for all general crime prevention activities and the Romanians the highest (41%). The UK was positioned at the high end with 37%.

13. *European Commission Report, ibid, p. 205 revealed more support from the 'less educated'* (June 2011).

REFERENCES

Accenture. (2013). Preparing police services for the future.

Bartlett, J., Miller, C., Crump, J., & Middleton, L. (2013). *Policing in an information age.* London: DEMOS.

Bichard, M. (2004). *The Bichard inquiry report: A public inquiry report on child protection procedures in Humberside Police and Cambridgeshire Constabulary, particularly the effectiveness of relevant intelligence-based record keeping, vetting practices since 1995 and information sharing with other agencies.* London: HMSO.

Boyd, D., & Crawford, K. (2012). Critical questions for Big Data: Provocations for a cultural, technological, and scholarly phenomenon. *Information, Communication, & Society, 15*(5), 662–679. Retrieved June 7, 2015, from http://www.danah.org/papers/2012/BigData-ICS-Draft.pdf

College of Policing. (2015). Leadership review: Interim report, Appendix 2.

Council Decision 2007/533/JHA.

Etzioni, A. (1999). *The limits of privacy.* New York: Basic Books.

European Commission. (2011, June). Eurobarometer 359 attitudes on data protection and electronic identity in the European Union Report.

European Commission Migration and Home Affairs Schengen Information System. (2015). Retrieved June 30, 2015, from http://ec.europa.eu/dgs/home-affairs/what-we-do/policies/borders-and-visas/schengen-information-system/index_en.htm

European Commission Press release. (2013, April 9). Questions and answers: Schengen Information System (SISII). Retrieved June 9, 2015, from www.europa.eu/rapid/press-release_MEMO-13-309_en.htm

Haggerty, K. D. (2012). Surveillance, crime and the police. In K. Ball, K. D. Haggerty, & D. Lyon (Eds.), *Routledge handbook of surveillance studies.* New York: Routledge Abingdon Oxon.

Hickey, H. (2015). Police oracle '*Huge backlog of criminal record checks*'. Retrieved April 8, 2015, from http://www.policeoracle.com/news/Huge-backlog-of-criminal-record-checks_87728

HMIC. (2011). The rules of engagement: Report into the August 2011 disorder.

HMIC. (2013). "Mistakes were made" HMIC's review into the allegations and intelligence material concerning Jimmy Savile between 1964 and 2012 (HMIC 978-1-78246-111-1).

HMIC. (2014a, October). Inspection of undercover policing in England and Wales.

HMIC. (2014b, June). Strategic policing requirement: An inspection of how police forces in England and Wales deal with threats of a large-scale incident (including criminal attack).

HMIC. (2014c, November). *State of policing: The annual assessment of policing in England and Wales 2013/14.* London: HMIC.

HMIC. (2015a, March). Rape monitoring groups: Digests and data 2013/14.

HMIC. (2015b, March). An inspection of the National Crime Agency.

HMIC. (2015c, July). In harm's way: The role of the police in keeping children safe.
HMIC. (2015d, July). Building the picture: An inspection of police information management (HMIC 978-1-78246-817-2).
Home Office. (2013). National DND Database Strategy Board Annual Report 2012–2013.
Home Office. (2014, March 31). Police workforce numbers, England and Wales.
House of Commons Science and Technology Committee. (2014). *Responsible use of Data 2014 Fourth report of Session 2014-2015 (HC 245)*. London: The Stationary Office.
Independent Chief Inspector of Borders and Immigration. (2013). Exporting the border? An inspection of e-borders, October 2012–March 2013.
Ipsos MORI. (2014, May). Privacy and personal data: Poll conducted by Ipsos MORI for the Joseph Rowntree Reform Trust, Ipsos MORI/Joseph Rowntree Reform Trust Limited.
Kitchin, R. (2014). *The data revolution: Big data, open data, data infrastructures and their consequences*. London: Sage.
Olesker, A. (2012). *Big Data solutions for law enforcement*. CLO Labs.
Omand, D., Bartlett, J., & Miller, C. (2012). *#Intelligence*. London: Demos.
Posner, R. (2006). *Not a suicide pact: The constitution in a time of national emergency*. New York: Oxford University Press.
Regulation (EC) No. 1986/2006.
Regulation (EC) No. 1987/2006.
S and Marper v UK. (2008). App No. 30562/04.
Sciencewise Expert Resource Centre. (2014, April). Big data: Public views on the collection, sharing and use of personal data by governments and companies (Version 1).
Sheptycki, J. (2004). Organizational pathologies in police intelligence systems: Some contributions to the lexicon of intelligence-led policing. *European Journal of Criminology Volume, 1*(3), 307–332.
Stanier, I. (2013). *Contemporary organisational pathologies in police information sharing: New contributions to Sheptycki's lexicon of intelligence led policing*. Unpublished Doctorate.
Weinfass, I. (2015). Police oracle '*GMP to review 11,000 firearms licences*'. Retrieved April 24, 2015, from http://www.policeoracle.com/news/GMP-to-review-11,000-firearms-licences_87971

Sociotechnical Imaginaries of Big Data: Commercial Satellite Imagery and Its Promise of Speed and Transparency

Philipp Olbrich and Nina Witjes

Abstract Geospatial Big Data is still a moving issue that is constantly contested and shaped by a multitude of actors and technological developments. Olbrich and Witjes carve out the sociotechnical imaginaries of the techno-political, analytical and security implications of geospatial Big Data development amongst the remote-sensing community. Predominantly, notions of condensed temporality and transparency permeate these visions and imagined futures. The community foresees that a constant influx of Earth observation data will replace current limits on availability and access; that epistemic practices evolve into machine–human synergies of accelerated processes of analysis; and that security policy needs to respond to a new sense of urgency as a result of increasingly predictive modes of operation.

Keywords Big Data • Earth observation • Geospatial information technologies • Sociotechnical imaginaries • Satellite imagery • Transparency • Machine–human interaction • Science and technology

P. Olbrich (✉) • N. Witjes
Department of International Relations and International Organization,
University of Groningen, Netherlands

115
A. Bunnik et al. (eds.), *Big Data Challenges*,
DOI 10.1057/978-1-349-94885-7_10

INTRODUCTION

Geospatial information technologies have undergone substantial technological and political transformations over the last decade and are used to
support decision-making in various policy fields. Civil society actors and
international organisations increasingly employ geospatial information
technologies—previously an exclusive state domain—such as remote sens-
ing, satellite navigation and internet mapping technologies to assess and
highlight security concerns (for example nuclear proliferation, natural disasters or human rights violations). In all these areas, commercial operators,
crowdsourcing initiatives and Non-Governmental Organisations (NGOs)
have substantially changed the application of Earth observation data in
terms of quality, quantity and access. Nowadays, millions of square kilometres of high-resolution satellite imagery are produced on a daily basis,
which poses novel opportunities and challenges for state as well as non-
state actors. To illustrate, the biggest commercial provider, DigitalGlobe,
can draw on an archive of more than 5 billion sq. kilometres of high-resolution imagery and currently adds another billion each year.

More generally, Big Data has received attention amongst social scientists in recent years (Chandler 2015; Craglia and Shanley 2015; Lee and
Kang 2015; Mainzer 2014; Reichert 2014; Boyd and Crawford 2012).
Mayer-Schönberger and Cukier (2013) have outlined three major shifts
in Big Data analytics that will alter our understanding of its impact on
society. First, the growing amount of data might allow for n=all analyses
of particular phenomena and render sampling obsolete. Second, Big Data
will change the ways we deal with exactitude and will support forecasting
of general trends and gaining new insights, especially on the macro level.
Third, researchers expect a shift from a focus on causal relations to correlations within the data, or, in a nutshell, 'Big Data is about what, not why'
(Mayer-Schönberger and Cukier 2013, p. 14). At the same time, although
there are quite a few current 'Big Data stories' around, it is still a moving
issue that is up for negotiation, constantly contested and shaped by a multitude of actors and technological developments.

Assessing how international relations scholars approach Big Data,
Chandler (2015) finds that discussions mainly revolve around pragmatic
opportunities for the improvement of research and knowledge through
the use of Big Data analytics. Questions have been raised about how Big
Data can contribute to problem solving and timely responses in cases
of disaster or conflict as well as to health and environmental questions.

Against this background, the general imaginary of Big Data is one in which production and consumption of knowledge and governance are not separated anymore; causal understandings lose relevance, as it is possible to adapt to 'real-time appearances of the world, without necessarily understanding them' (Chandler 2015, p. 843). Zwitter and Hadfield (2014, p. 2) refer to this state of contestation and projected technological capability captured in the unknown future of Big Data by pointing to the present. They draw attention to still-unresolved issues of ethical responsibility, personal security and privacy as well as a missing code of conduct for governing Big Data. Generally speaking, narratives of Big Data are most often drawing on, building and cultivating *visions and imagined future developments.*

Against this background, we ask how actors in the field of satellite imagery analysis envision the ways geospatial Big Data is going to develop in the future and how they are going to make use of it. How do they assess the socio-technological challenges and opportunities regarding changes in their working process and the associated political implications?

To answer these questions, we will make use of the concept of sociotechnical imaginaries that grasps how social actors relate to future technological developments. Jasanoff and Kim (2009, p. 120) defined national sociotechnical imaginaries as 'collectively imagined forms of social life and social order reflected in the design and fulfilment of nation-specific scientific and/or technological projects. Imaginaries, in this sense, at once describe attainable futures and prescribe futures that states believe ought to be attained.' The concept is often used to investigate issues situated at the intersection of political science and science and technology studies, such as bilateral cooperation in green technologies (Müller and Witjes 2014, p. 50), governance of bioenergy and biofuels (Levidow and Papaioannou 2014; Levidow and Papaioannou 2013), development research (Smith 2009), or how the Internet is envisioned to transgress boundaries of both knowledge orders and physical geographies (Felt 2014). In addition to the initial focus (Jasanoff and Kim 2009), the concept is compatible with various units of analysis beyond the nation state but can also address common visions and narratives of how our techno-political world should be socially ordered as articulated by expert groups, NGOs, companies, or foundations.

To understand how and in what ways the satellite imagery community is crafting a sociotechnical imaginary of Big Data, we are building our empirical investigation on a series of interviews with mainly U.S.-based satellite imagery analysts as well as members of the international geospatial intelligence community. Moreover, we conducted a document analysis of policy strategies, official statements, reports, websites and public interviews that deal with the techno-political future of satellite imagery as geospatial Big Data.

THE FUTURE OF GEOSPATIAL BIG DATA

The following empirical section is divided into three interrelated parts. First, we reconstruct the ways in which the advancement of commercial satellite imagery is envisioned by the community of its producers and users. Second, we show how these actors anticipate challenges and opportunities derived from the introduction of geospatial Big Data analytics. Third, we trace how these actors refer to the future impact and meaning of Big Data on the level of security policy.

ORBITING DOVES: THE COMMERCIALISATION OF EARTH OBSERVATION

Whilst governments are upgrading their Earth observation capabilities, radical change is happening in the private satellite technology sector. Here, corporations have increasingly filled in the blanks of government remote-sensing data over the past years. In the U.S. context, DigitalGlobe assumes a particular role in the meshwork of private-public cooperation for generating and analysing satellite imagery and reportedly makes more than 50 % of its revenue from U.S. government contracts (Roy and Raghavan 2014). However, more players, like Skybox or PlanetLabs, are bound to enter this growing market and add to the crowding of low-earth orbits. DigitalGlobe might still capture commercial imagery with the highest resolution, but the companies mentioned put forward a vision of condensed temporality. That is, their articulated ambition is to revisit and basically image the globe every single day (IP 10:1)[1] and thereby create unprecedented amounts of Earth observation data. Furthermore, they are framing this data future as a contribution to transparency in the realm of diverse fields such as mining, logistics, agriculture, economic and urban planning, or environmental monitoring (Kearns 2015; Scanlon 2014). Both the co-founders of Skybox and PlanetLabs present their motivation or mission to launch their own satellite constellation and analytics as to 'provide global transparency' in a timely manner (Berkenstock 2013).

Also, PlanetLabs calls its micro satellites 'doves', relating its technological system to a strong pacifist symbol that is often considered a peaceful messenger. In doing so, they present their micro satellites as carrying out a 'humanitarian mission' by creating real-time data of the whole planet for virtually everyone (Marshall 2014) for the sake of data democracy and transparency.

The unstoppable proliferation of geospatial Big Data is not only imagined as increasing general transparency and democratised access, but occurs in real time (Marshall 2014; IP 9:5). Depending on, amongst other things, the geographical area of interest and (economic) relevance for commercial imagery providers, analysts have to wait days or even weeks for new satellite imagery to be captured. Lengthy waiting is believed to become unnecessary as technological improvement is going to make real-time analysis a common factor in the future, so analysts and others with access to geospatial information become a part of a kinetic environment (IP 9:5; IP 1:89). This improvement in so-called temporal resolution is also believed to provide a remedy for certain technical, institutional and interpretational uncertainties related to satellite imagery analysis.[2] For example, daily or even more frequent coverage is believed to better identify certain camouflage, concealment and deception (CCD) activities; alleviate detrimental weather conditions, such as cloud cover or moisture; and provide more in-depth pattern-of-life information on objects and people on the ground (IP 1:89).

FEEDING THE ALGORITHM: HUMAN–MACHINE INTERACTIONS

The predominant narratives of condensed temporality and transparency are prevalent in the area of knowledge production based on satellite imagery, albeit in slightly different flavours. Transparency is often characterised as a consequence of increased commercial competition and growing amounts of satellite data. However, increased data leads to pressures for the analysis, as the continuous influx of geospatial Big Data needs to be handled in a fashion that exploits the data to a maximum, meaning that 'you can't operate with the same paradigm anymore' (McCarthy 2015b). Government and non-governmental analysts alike point out that the number of people capable of analysing imagery is very low compared to how much data needs to be analysed (IP 2:86). As a consequence, there is widespread agreement amongst analysts, developers and government officials that machine-learning algorithms will become a major part of future satellite imagery analysis in order to account for the rapidly growing amount of Earth observation data.

More conservative expectations raised in the narrative of Big Data are automatic object identification and quantification. In a broad sense, identification and quantification refer to feeding an algorithm with large amounts of Earth observation data so that it automatically highlights, for example, roads, water and energy networks; refugee camps; or places suitable for nuclear reactors (IP 2:87; IP 9:3). In particular, for most non-governmental actors (that is, NGOs or researchers), even these analytical tools are still in early development due to limited resources of money, programming skills and data. However, interviewees attribute a great future value to these capabilities, which are expected to support them in coping 'with large areas of interest and time pressure' (IP 9:4) and therefore deemed 'critical for going forward' (IP 9:3).

These expectations have to be understood in a discursive context that sees human epistemic capacity as reaching its limits when it comes to geospatial Big Data. For many, using automatic object identification and quantification promises to increase human knowledge about the world in unprecedented ways, because it surpasses human capacities (Safford 2015; Berkenstock 2013). At the same time, these hopes are accompanied by an implicit warning that not using the superior power of Big Data analytics would amount to a waste of opportunities to acquire relevant knowledge.

Satellite imagery providers are already planning to accommodate analysts' needs by building large databases that allow customers to access them externally and run their own algorithms (IP 10:17; IP 10:10). So rather than data being sent to the analyst, the analyst goes to the data. In addition to the growing availability of Earth observation data, the 'Analysis Technology Vision for 2020' of the US National Geospatial-Intelligence Agency (NGA) also points toward a shift in time management. The NGA foresees that analysts will, to a lesser extent, grapple with raw data (that is, satellite images themselves), but instead spend more time on the interpretation of broader relationships whilst being part of a semi-automated environment. In short, algorithms initiate and support the transition 'from a forensic-based to a model-based approach' to analysis (NGA 2014, pp. 3–4). This development is also believed to allow for faster, near real-time analyses and constantly running surveillance of data.

A central aspect of how stakeholders imagine geospatial Big Data analytics is that it is envisioned to be a 'joint effort between humans and computers' (NGA 2014, p. 6). This human–machine collaboration would require that analysts learn new skills, such as validating computer-generated results and integrating them into a meaningful context, thus acknowledging certain limits of the human capacity to adequately analyse the growing amount of Earth Observation data whilst simultaneously pointing out that human interference is—as of today—still necessary because 'nothing to date matches the perception of the human brain' (Barrington 2014). Analysts assign to automated tools an operational support function to deal with the large amounts of imagery and to tell the analyst where to look more closely (IP 9:4). The vision pertains, for example, to situations of monitoring an active conflict area. A sophisticated algorithm fed with satellite imagery might lead a human analyst to spontaneous refugee camps or troop movements in near real-time, and the analyst then can classify and interpret what he or she sees in more detail before forwarding his or her analysis to relevant decision-makers or audiences. This development alludes to the vision of geospatial predictive analytics, which will be dealt with in the subsequent section.

Current practices of crowdsourcing satellite imagery are a prime example and manifestation of the envisioned computer-human collaboration that is also designed to deal with time pressure. Platforms such as Tomnod make use of volunteers who help to handle large amounts of geospatial data and imagery. In specific instances, lay people were mobilised to map damages after the earthquake in Nepal in 2015 or identify military objects and large crowds during the conflict in Syria. This development also illustrates the speed of satellite imagery, as the crowd was harnessed in order to provide a rapid and timely response (IP 2:9). Moreover, it should be noted that the tagging of imagery by volunteers at scale was not a backup plan of DigitalGlobe, which owns Tomnod. Instead, the company used the crowd to increase profits and improve its machine-learning systems for automated satellite imagery analysis 'until artificial intelligence could catch up to fully automate the process' (Meier 2015, p. 120). Again, a certain temporality is evoked as an important element in framing the narrative of Big Data analytics in that the technology is expected to catch up at some point in time.

Risks, Promises and Pushing Boundaries: Expected Political Implications

Satellite imagery analysis is already a common source for informing decisions on issues such as treaty verification, natural disaster response, humanitarian action, or military intervention. Therefore, how imagery experts envision the impact and consequences of advanced geospatial Big Data analytics for political action is a central element to the respective imaginary. The interviews revealed a largely unambiguous view of the technological progress of analytical tools to exploit large amounts of satellite imagery as predetermined, irreversible and useful for decision-making (IP 8:5). Since the database is set to grow in quality and quantity, the future use of Earth observation data is envisioned to comprise more political areas, and even become a factor in determining a political agenda itself. Beyond its function as additional information for an existing problem, it will be asked, 'What can we do with that imagery?' (IP 3:55), a question that will open new issues or define the direction of (new) discourses. The NGA acknowledges that pushing the technical boundaries to provide unique geospatial intelligence and support proactive decision-making 'requires some acceptance of risk' (NGA 2014, p. 9). However, simultaneously, it asserts, without providing specifics, that this 'risk' will be somehow alleviated through the further commercialisation of data.

Adding to the notion of a shifting temporality, geospatial Big Data is seen as useful for the preparation for, pre-definition of and anticipation of events on the ground. The vision is to go beyond the current response system. Nowadays, in the case of natural disasters, crowdsourcing initiatives or OpenStreet mappers are drawn on to create up-to-date and accurate maps to support the work of relief organisations. In these instances, a commercial provider and/or government can choose to release imagery to the public for a limited amount of time to enable crisis response. However, the future vision of geospatial Big Data is to make use of the stored and incoming imagery to map the whole globe in a systematic fashion so that the information is ready to build a 'a more proactive basis as opposed to a reaction to a crisis' (IP10:19). Yet, for most members of the Earth observation community, the imaginary does not stop at the level of preparedness and transparency, but is set to venture into the area of prediction. In political terms, the value of predictive information and scenario-based approaches is seen in the opportunity for preventive policy.

Instead of monitoring and documenting human rights violations, the goal is 'to prevent these things from happening in the first place' (IP 10:11; see also NGA 2014, p. 8). In one case, DigitalGlobe cooperated with the Enough Project to use predictive geospatial Big Data analytics to combat elephant poaching in the Garamba National Park by using geospatial data to identify high-risk poaching areas to assist local park rangers in anticipating and pre-empting ivory trafficking (DigitalGlobe 2015). Speed is, again, invoked as an important notion for the effective use of geospatial Big

Data by non-state as well as governmental actors. Duncan McCarthy of the NGA, for example, foresees an increasing reliance of his agency on automatically pre-analysed data and likens this ability to the movie 'Minority Report' before presenting his vision of being 'ahead of the news' on a constant basis (McCarthy 2015a). Some analysts raised certain political and ethical issues when real-time or predictive information is made public. In active conflict scenarios, they called for more reflection and caution about this real-time capacity in order to prevent vulnerable people from becoming more endangered. They also provided military information to parties to a conflict (IP 9:6; IP 9:5). However, the great majority of interviewees generally appreciated the value of real-time or even predictive geospatial information for political purposes.

CONCLUSIONS

One underlying point of reference in the accounts of geospatial Big Data is the advent of a new space age heralded by the interplay of profound changes in three separate but mutually entangled areas: the techno-political development of Earth observation, the changing ways of knowledge production, and the policy impact and governance of geospatial Big Data. Following this trichotomy, we have outlined how satellite imagery contributes to the formation of a specific sociotechnical imaginary of geospatial Big Data. The two notions that are most prevalent in the accounts of satellite imagery providers, government officials and imagery analysts are condensed temporality and increasing transparency.

First, on the technological side, the geospatial community expects the current limitations of commercial satellite imagery in quality, currency and availability will be replaced by a constant influx of Earth observation data. This influx will come about mainly through growing market competition, leading to daily imaging—often likened to data democracy—on a global scale. However, despite the narrative of the ever-increasing availability of and easy access to commercial satellite imagery, geospatial experts in governments and the defence industry point out that the availability of data is still amongst their biggest challenges (DGI 2015, 2014). It is not clear whether questionable availability is due to the lack of data or difficulties in access (for example, due to limited budgets), but geospatial Big Data as a reliant means of enhanced transparency has not been realised yet for them.

Second, geospatial Big Data is imagined to alter the work process of human analysts in two sequential ways so as to live up to expectations of increased transparency and speed. In order to overcome the task of sufficiently exploiting the growing amount of Earth observation data, analysts deem it necessary to invest in and develop sophisticated machine-learning systems. The epistemic practices are then expected to change in synergy with those algorithms, in that analysts become a part of an accelerated process of analysis and integrate automated results into a broader context. However, satellite imagery analysts do not envision fully automated imagery analysis, but highlight the importance of human involvement and sensitivity to context. Whilst other accounts speak of the agency of data or the meaninglessness of 'the subject/object divide of modernist knowledge production' (Chandler 2015, p. 847), a complete computerisation of analysis is rarely articulated and imagined in the satellite imagery community, which still envisages the human analysts as playing an important role.

Last, implications for security policy are mainly imagined as a consequence of increasing data availability and predictive methods of analysis. Although the current state of the art is dominated by monitoring and documenting, geospatial Big Data analytics are envisioned to allow for more preventive policy measures. The increasing transparency of developments on the ground is imagined to bring about a new sense of urgency, as one is empowered to (pre)act on to predicted events and, potentially, prevent them. Still, the general narrative of geospatial Big Data as increasing transparency rarely includes the present political and legal limitations. For example, US commercial imagery providers operate under national law, which means that the government can lock down the free distribution of imagery and interfere with commercial operations if it fears its national security interests are being compromised. Rather, it is envisioned that the techno-political development can do away with these regulations, which are framed as limiting transparency.

We have outlined a collective vision of the future in which geospatial Big Data is imagined to become an 'everyday reality' for the satellite imagery community. This vision, in turn, would mean that it also becomes an everyday reality for those being observed who have been strikingly absent in the imaginary.

NOTES

1. This refers to specific interview partners who will be quoted anonymously by mutual agreement.
2. For an analysis on uncertainties of satellite imagery analysis and the legitimacy of knowledge claims in the field of international security, see Witjes and Olbrich (2015).

REFERENCES

Barrington, L. (2014). Crowdsourcing satellite imagery. Retrieved August 11, 2015, from http://eijournal.com/print/articles/crowdsourcing

Berkenstock, D. (2013). The world is one big dataset. Now, how to photograph it... Retrieved August 13, 2015, from www.ted.com/talks/dan_berkenstock_ the_world_is_one_big_dataset_now_how_to_photograph_it? language=en

Boyd, D., & Crawford, K. (2012). Critical questions for Big Data: Provocations for a cultural, technological, and scholarly phenomenon. *Information, Communication & Society, 15*(5), 662–679.

Chandler, D. (2015). A world without causation: Big Data and the coming of age of posthumanism. *Millennium, 43*(3), 833–851.

Craglia, M., & Shanley, L. (2015). Data democracy—increased supply of geospatial information and expanded participatory processes in the production of data. *International Journal of Digital Earth, 8*, 1–15. doi:10.1080/17538947 .2015.1008214.

DGI [Defence Geospatial Intelligence]. (2014). DGI 2014 industry survey. Retrieved August 14, 2015, from http://dgi.wbresearch.com/media/ 1001380/33013.pdf

DGI [Defence Geospatial Intelligence]. (2015). DGI 2015 industry survey. Retrieved August 14, 2015, from http://dgi.wbresearch.com/media/1001380/27235.pdf

DigitalGlobe. (2015). Poachers without borders: New satellite imaging and predictive mapping to empower park rangers and combat ivory traffickers in Garamba National Park. Retrieved August 14, 2015, from www.enoughproject.org/files/PoachersWithoutBorders_28Jan2015.pdf

Felt, U. (2014). Sociotechnical imaginaries of "the internet", digital health information and the making of citizen-patients. *Vienna*. Retrieved August 13, 2015, from http://sts.univie.ac.at/fileadmin/user_upload/dep_sciencestudies/pdf_ files/Preprints/Felt_citizen-patient_01.pdf

Jasanoff, S., & Kim, S.-H. (2009). Containing the atom: Sociotechnical imaginaries and nuclear power in the United States and South Korea. *Minerva, 47*(2), 119–146.

Kearns, J. (2015). Satellite images show economies growing and shrinking in real time. Retrieved August 13, 2015, from www.bloomberg.com/news/ features/2015-07-08/satellite-images-show-economies-growing-and-shrinking-in-real-time

Lee, J.-G., & Kang, M. (2015). Geospatial Big Data: Challenges and opportunities. *Big Data Research, 2*(2), 74–81.

Levidow, L., & Papaioannou, T. (2013). State imaginaries of the public good: Shaping UK innovation priorities for bioenergy. *Environmental Science and Policy, 30*(1), 36–49.

Levidow, L., & Papaioannou, T. (2014). UK biofuel policy: Envisaging sustainable biofuels, shaping institutions and futures. *Environment and Planning A*, *46*(2), 280–298.

Mainzer, K. (2014). *Die Berechnung der Welt: Von der Weltformel zu Big Data*. Munich: C.H. Beck.

Marshall, W. (2014). Tiny satellites show us the Earth as it changes in near-real-me. Retrieved August 13, 2015, from www.ted.com/talks/will_marshall_teeny_tiny_satellites_that_photograph_the_entire_planet_every_day?language=en

Mayer-Schönberger, V., & Cukier, K. (2013). *Big Data: Die revolution, die unser Leben verändern wird*. Munich: Redline.

McCarthy, D. (2015a). FEF Big Data future vision NGA April 2015. Retrieved August 14, 2015, from www.youtube.com/watch?v=UNWo0_NMd8A

McCarthy, D. (2015b). FEF Big Data progress NGA April 2015. Retrieved August 13, 2015, from www.youtube.com/watch?v=y_DApC9vQVY

Meier, P. (2015). *Digital humanitarians: How Big Data is changing the face of humanitarian response*. Boca Raton: CRC Press.

Müller, R., & Witjes, N. (2014). Of red threads and green dragons. Austrian sociotechnical imaginaries about STI cooperation with China. In M. Mayer, M. Carpes, & R. Knoblich (Eds.), *The global politics of science and technology* (pp. 47–65). Heidelberg: Springer.

NGA [National Geosptial-Intelligence Agency]. (2014). 2020 analysis technology plan. Retrieved August 13, 2015, from www.nga.mil/MediaRoom/PressReleases/Documents/NGA_Analysis_Tech_Plan.pdf

Reichert, R. (2014). *Big Data: Analysen zum digitalen Wandel von Wissen, Macht und Ökonomie*. Bielefeld: transcript.

Roy, A., & Raghavan, M. (2014). DigitalGlobe eyes $400 million market for high-res images. Retrieved August 13, 2015, from www.reuters.com/article/2014/05/23/us-digitalglobe-cfo-idUSBREA4M08920140523

Safford, M. (2015). A startup wants to track everything from shoppers to corn yields using satellite imagery. Retrieved August 13, 2015, from www.smithsonianmag.com/innovation/startup-wants-to-track-everything-from-shoppers-to-corn-yields-using-satellite-imagery-180954776/?no-ist

Scanlon, J. (2014). There's more to the small Skybox satellite than meets the eye. Much, much more. Retrieved August 13, 2015, from http://ideas.ted.com/theres-more-to-the-small-skybox-satellite-than-meets-the-eye-much-much-ore/

Smith, E. (2009). Imaginaries of development: The Rockefeller Foundation and rice research. *Science as Culture*, *18*(4), 461–482.

Witjes, N., & Olbrich, P. (2015). Reflecting security knowledge: The legitimacy of satellite imagery analysis in international affairs. In C. Günay & J. Pospisil (Eds.), *Legitimacy beyond normative orders?* (pp. 115–128). Vienna: Facultas.

Zwitter, A. J., & Hadfield, A. (2014). Governing Big Data. *Politics and Governance*, *2*(1), 1–3.

CHAPTER 11

Using Big Data to Achieve Food Security

Bryce Evans

Abstract This chapter considers the implications and limitations of Big Data in helping to achieve global food security. It highlights how Big Data is already being used to inform humanitarian food security initiatives. The chapter reflects on the United Nations' Global Pulse initiative, which gathers real-time data and feedback on policy responses to humanitarian crises to try to improve practice amongst development organisations and make food security better. The chapter also highlights the limitations of Big Data's role in enhancing food security; such limitations include the unpredictability of human behaviour, societal and ancestral contexts, and the potential for data-informed mass perception to be misleading. The harnessing of Big Data to improve food security may also encounter resistance from political and economic interest groups.

Keywords Big Data • Food security • Hunger • Food availability • Food access • Food use • United Nations • Global Pulse • Humanitarian crises • NGOs

B. Evans (✉)
Department of History and Politics, Liverpool Hope University, UK

© The Editor(s) (if applicable) and The Author(s) 2016   127
A. Bunnik et al. (eds.), *Big Data Challenges*,
DOI 10.1057/978-1-349-94885-7_11

INTRODUCTION

Global hunger: we have heard the grim statistics so often that their clout has diminished. Nonetheless, they are worth repeating. Almost a billion people in the world do not have enough food to eat (United Nations Food and Agriculture Organisation 2012). Worldwide, poor nutrition is responsible for around half of all deaths in children under five (Horton and Lo 2013). Hunger kills more people every year than AIDS, malaria, and tuberculosis combined (United Nations Food and Agriculture Organisation 2012). As detailed elsewhere in this publication, Big Data has epoch-defining potential. But can its use help alleviate hunger—that most fundamental and historically persistent human problem—and, in doing so, bolster global food security?

Food security, as defined by the World Food Summit of 1996, exists 'when all people at all times have access to sufficient, safe, nutritious food to maintain a healthy and active life'. It comprises three pillars: *food availability* (having sufficient quantities of food available on a consistent basis), *food access* (having sufficient resources to obtain appropriate foods for a nutritious diet), and *food use* (the appropriate use of food based on knowledge of basic nutrition and care, as well as adequate water and sanitation) (Rome: UN 1996). Such big goals, naturally, present no easy solutions. This article, therefore, addresses the implications and limitations of Big Data in helping to achieve global food security.

GLOBAL PULSE

For all the caution amongst analysts about Big Data, its use is already informing humanitarian food security initiatives of the twenty-first century. Since 2009, the United Nations (UN) has been running what it calls its 'Global Pulse' initiative. Global Pulse is an innovation scheme launched by the Executive Office of the UN Secretary-General in response to the need for more timely information to track and monitor global socioeconomic crises such as famine, droughts, and conflicts.

Global Pulse constitutes an international collaborative recognition that Big Data offers important humanitarian opportunities. It enables UN agencies to gain real-time feedback on how well policy responses to the often-vicious circle of humanitarian crises are working. Its aim is to improve practice amongst development organisations and, ultimately, to achieve tangible results in achieving improved food security (UN Global Pulse 2014).

In practice, Global Pulse functions as a network of 'innovation labs,' where research on Big Data for development is coordinated. In these laboratories, teams of researchers and analysts use data mining and real-time data analytics to spot looming food crises. According to a recent report by the UN Office for the Coordination of Humanitarian Affairs, data mined at these labs has the potential to strengthen early warning systems for food insecurity.

For example, the Global Pulse lab in Jakarta found that a critical mass of tweets sent from 2010 to 2011 in Indonesia (a developing country which has the highest number of tweets per head in the world) reflected the impact of rising food prices and inflation on the population. This Twitter traffic served as an indicator of the 2012 global food crisis, which witnessed spikes in the price of staple foods across the world. The lab was able to monitor consumer price indexes for basic foodstuffs through food keywords people used online and compared this discussion to past data (Maclean 2013). When correlations between social media conversations on food-related topics and official inflation data started to emerge, Jakarta's Global Pulse analysts were able to flag the likely local impacts of the crisis and deploy resources accordingly.

In 2014 Global Pulse implemented over 25 joint data innovation projects worldwide. Implementation involved the analysis of over 350 million tweets. Global Pulse (2014) also regularly states the case for the concept of 'data philanthropy', arguing that private sector holders of big data can and should release such information for the common good. In doing so, it has sought to back up UN General Secretary Ban Ki-Moon's 2014 call for countries to harness the data revolution to achieve sustainable development.

FOOD AND THE 'INDUSTRIAL REVOLUTION' IN DATA

As the 'Global Pulse' model illustrates, the benefits of using free, real-time digital information to inform food policy seem obvious. Rather than relying on outdated statistics, we now have the revolutionary ability to gain a comprehensive picture of the well-being of populations. Although the broader movement has been termed an 'industrial revolution in data', the opportunities are not confined to first world or even to industrialised economies (Letouzé 2012, p. 7).

Whilst many people in the most food-insecure regions of the world still do not use Twitter or other social media platforms, developing countries have experienced a marked expansion in the use of digital devices, principally due to the greater affordability of mobile phones. There were over five billion mobile phones in use around the world in 2010, of which 80% were located in developing countries (Google Fusion Tables 2013).

In a future world in which an expansion in population is predicted to move hand-in-hand with greater global volatility, Big Data could be a crucial asset. The food price spikes of 2007–2008, which resulted in rioting in over forty countries, were felt hardest in developing nations. According to the Organisation for Economic Co-operation and Development (OECD), such instances of food-related conflict are likely to occur with increased frequency, with 'disruptive shocks to the global economy' becoming 'more frequent and caus[ing] greater economic and societal hardship' (OECD 2011). Therefore, the enhanced ability to track real-time instances of food insecurity could be vital in saving lives, particularly in the most food insecure areas of the world—sub-Saharan Africa, Asia, and the Pacific—where the use of digital devices is taking off.

The digital data revolution has the potential to complement existing food early warning systems operated by NGOs and UN agencies. Such systems tend to focus on climate shocks in rural areas. When taken alongside the traditional climatic warnings, large-scale data mined from mobile phone usage will deepen understanding of regional food insecurity. Factors such as an increase in traffic on mobile trading networks on livestock, the depletion of mobile banking funds or an upsurge in tweets about food shortage and prices will, it is anticipated, help agencies gain a better handle on the nature of a crisis in a short and relevant period of time (Letouzé 2013, p. 14).

The use of Big Data to inform early warning mechanisms such as the UN Food and Agriculture Organization's Quarterly Early Warning Bulletin is now well established. Data from the UN's Global Information and Early Warning System (which offers an online food-price tracking mechanism) and the Emergency Prevention System for Animal Health (which utilises disease intelligence and surveillance) are used in the compilation of the bulletin (UN FAO Early Warning Bulletin, April–June 2015).

Underlining this point, few analysts of traditional economic and political data predicted the scale of the so-called 'Arab Spring' of 2011 onwards. After all, annual growth rates in many Arab economies were above the world average (Breisinger 2011). But a key factor in the violent uprisings that sent dictators toppling across the Maghreb was that many people in the wider Arab world *perceived* their standard of living to be unsatisfactory (Ecker 2013). One constant factor in this perception of dissatisfaction was—and is—food insecurity. Revolutions should not be reduced to mere 'rebellions of the belly', caused only by upsurges in the price of bread; in Egypt, for example, the state traditionally responded to food riots by 'buying off' the protestors (for instance, by increasing food subsidies). The overriding point is that the rising price of food is often the catalyst for turning a welter of other grievances into violent conflict. Therefore, Big Data analysis, gathered more quickly and emanating from less 'traditional' statistical sources, could well have provided a more complex *yet simultaneously clearer* indication that a major disruptive shock to the Arab world was imminent.

LIMITATIONS

Raising the prospect of Big Data as a boon to food security brings with it questions about its limitations in this realm. When 26-year-old Tunisian street vendor Tarek al-Tayeb Mohamed Bouazizi set himself on fire on 17 December 2010, he had little idea that he would ignite the 'Arab Spring'. It is significant that the authorities had unfairly harassed Bouazizi's fruit and vegetable business, confiscating his weighing devices and humiliating him, thereby simultaneously tipping the scales of the delicate moral economy of food supply in the developing world.

This grievance, alongside a raft of other concerns, shaped Bouazizi's desperate act and its spiralling consequences. As mentioned above, mass trends in data from digital devices may have provided an indication that a major disruptive shock was likely in the Arab world. But even the most sophisticated proprietary algorithm cannot always predict the inherently unpredictable when it comes to human behaviour and an individual's social and psychological makeup. Furthermore, mass perception about issues as basic as the price of bread or even its taste can be misleading. Sentiment analysis (or opinion mining) has its clear boundaries.

For food security, such consideration of human agency demands primacy. When food security is conceptualised in its most basic sense—the absence of starvation—one of the chief concerns about Big Data, namely its infringement on personal privacy, appears something of a 'first world problem'. When human lives are at stake, it is tempting to believe that the mobilisation of all available data resources, regardless of how they are gathered, trumps all other concerns. But the clamour for liberty, human rights, transparency, and pluralism has been a hallmark of democratic movements in the developing world, where the concentration of masses of people in protest has had huge implications for food security. Mobs might be angry but they are also thinking, complex entities and may not take kindly to what they perceive as outside agents perpetrating mass infringements on their liberty, albeit their digital liberty.

This possibility raises further questions about the use of Big Data to support conventional models of food aid by 'philanthropic' outside actors. According to an increasingly vocal body of academic opinion, the provision of major food aid along established lines might not be the solution (Nunn and Qian 2012). In fact, some say that sending food to conflict zones to ease food security is not a good idea, as doing so merely prolongs civil war and, with it, the vicious circle of conflict and hunger.

NGOs working to alleviate the food insecurity caused by Somalia's civil wars of the 1990s soon found that they were forced to discreetly subcontract armed clan militia leaders in order to effectively distribute food (Kilcullen 2013). Similarly, in countries or areas (for instance, Sudan's Darfur region) currently experiencing the gravest food insecurity (which is, in every case, exacerbated by conflict), the problem is complicated by inter-tribal rivalry. The situation on the ground is often shaped by deeply powerful ancestral forces that outside actors, even when using all the technological and economic muscle at their disposal, struggle to negotiate.

Mobile phones are used in the developing world to buy and sell food, to transfer money, to search for work, and to monitor food stock levels. But compared to the data deluge of the developed world, there are limits to what information can be garnered. Big Data detailing mobile-banking transactions may be useful in predicting food insecurity, yet, in many developing countries, people will have mobile phones but no bank accounts. The technological limitations of older mobile phones also ensure that user-generated content is less extensive than in the developed world. Moreover, in contrast to developing countries like Indonesia and Brazil with high internet penetration, in food-insecure conflict zones (such as Syria) the internet may be unavailable for lengthy periods (FAO/WFP 2013).

Big Data, Finance Capitalism, and Food Insecurity

In 2008, an archetypal historical problem returned with a rather loud bang. The food riot—with its attendant notions of moral economy—was witnessed across the globe. In that year, rioting in 48 countries was a consequence of bad harvests and a rise in the price of staple food (Bohstedt 2013). In Haiti, with angry crowds demanding cheaper rice, the country's prime minister was forced to resign. Similarly, with food price volatility linked to the state's plan to lease arable land to foreign concerns, the President of Madagascar was forced aside. In 2012, droughts again ensured a spike in world cereal prices and exacerbated ongoing conflicts in central Africa and Syria. At the time of writing, in places like Mali, the Democratic Republic of Congo, and Syria, refugee crises are compounding food crises.

Revolutions, wars, droughts, and other disruptive shocks to food security are age-old. Yet, when it comes to Big Data and food security, there is an insidious final factor to consider.

Global investors recently pulled out of the West African nation of Guinea-Bissau because data pointed to political volatility following a 2012 coup. With the withdrawal of support by lenders, state funding for basic nutrition and food security programmes collapsed. Likewise, the country's cashew nut export trade slumped. Because cashew nuts account for 90% of Guinea-Bissau's exports and 45% of its Gross Domestic Product (GDP), the miserable certainty of hunger now looms for the country's inhabitants (UN Office for the Coordination of Humanitarian Affairs 2013).

Guinea-Bissau provides just one example of the power of global finance's big players to alter national food security at a stroke. Not all companies are guilty of humanitarian oversight. MasterCard, for one, prides itself on its recently developed 'digital food', an electronic system where vouchers can be used in special World-Food-Programme approved shops to buy food (Business Life 2013). But amidst the 'industrial revolution in data', an obvious concern is the corporate use of Big Data to identify risks to investment when the outcome—as in Guinea-Bissau—seriously exacerbates food insecurity. In such cases, actors such as the European Union and NGOs often find themselves applying expensive and rather ineffective sticking plasters.

An added worry is the unsettling prospect of the corporate manipulation of data to justify often-dubious ends. This potential is a pressing concern in the age of Big Data, with information based on subjective data sets, such as opinion mining, taking its place beside more traditional econometric measures.

Commodity speculation, a capitalist phenomenon which first flowered in the Victorian era, remains a major contributor to extreme price volatility. Underlying the serious instances of food insecurity in 2008 was extortionate commodity speculation. As the Fairtrade movement has highlighted, cocoa was subjected to some of the worst excesses. A handful of investment firms were said to have 'stolen' the cocoa market in that year by suddenly driving cocoa prices up by over 44% (Institute for Agriculture and Trade Policy 2008, p. 6).

Today, commodity index-fund investors use Big Data to bundle contracts in the lucrative futures market. They do so by using a formula that weighs and tracks the prices of hundreds of commodities as a single financial instrument. Data is used to create a constant upward pressure on commodity prices. This momentum is interrupted only when profit is taken on the futures and options contracts. Profits are periodically 'rolled over' according to trading algorithms (Institute for Agriculture and Trade Policy 2008, p. 8). In such an unrelentingly profit-driven system, the global poor are, of course, of little concern and food insecurity is exacerbated.

Conclusions

Leveraging Big Data can improve food security by reducing delays in the gathering, processing, and diffusion of information, allowing more efficient, analytically-informed decision-making. In doing so, Big Data forms part of the toolkit of established assessments, such as the World Food Programme's Vulnerability Analysis and Mapping, that identify food-insecure populations. The use of Big Data, therefore, has the potential to bolster food security and, in some contexts, to take its place as the centrepiece of new initiatives to combat hunger.

Big Data's revolutionary potential in this realm, however, remains dependent on the will of international agencies and global powers to address the structural causes of global food insecurity. In the USA, the world's largest food-aid donor, the Obama administration's attempts to tackle the inefficiencies of food aid have faced the robust opposition of agribusinesses, NGOs, and shipping companies. Significant improvements to food security through the humanitarian harnessing of Big Data may come, then, but history has shown that change—in this field—comes slowly.

References

Bohstedt, J. (2013, July 12). (University of Tennessee, Knoxville) *The politics of provisions: The food riots of 2007–08 in Historical Contexts*. 82nd Anglo-American Conference of Historians, Institute of Historical Research.

Breisinger, C., Ecker, O., & Al-Riffai, P. (2011, May). *Economics of the Arab awakening: From revolution to transformation and food security*. Washington, DC: International Food Policy Research Institute.

Business Life. (2013, June 24). What I've learnt: Ann Cairns. Retrieved from http://businesslife.ba.com/People/What-Ive-Learnt/What-Ive-learnt-Ann-Cairns.html

Ecker, O. (2013, May 12). (interview) International Food Policy Research Institute, Washington, DC.

FAO/WFP. (2013, July 5). Crop and food security assessment mission to the Syrian Arab Republic. Rome: UN.

Google Fusion Tables. (2013). Retrieved May 2, 2013, from http://www.google.com/fusiontables/Home/

Horton, R., & Lo, S. (2013, June). Nutrition: A quintessential sustainable development goal. *The Lancet* (Lancet Early Online Publication).

Institute for Agriculture and Trade Policy. (2008). *Commodities market speculation: The risk to food security and agriculture.* Minneapolis: IATP.

Kilcullen, D. (2013, July 23). *Feral Cities,* broadcast on BBC Radio 4. Retrieved from http://www.bbc.co.uk/programmes/b0375p83

Letouzé, E. (2012). *Big Data for development: Challenges & opportunities* (p. 7). New York: UN. Retrieved April 2, 2013, from http://www.unglobalpulse.org/sites/default/files/BigDataforDevelopment-UNGlobalPulseJune2012.pdf

Letouzé, E. (2013). *Big Data for Development,* p. 14. Retrieved April 2, 2013, from http://www.unglobalpulse.org/sites/default/files/BigDataforDevelopment-UNGlobalPulseJune2012.pdf

MacLean, D. (2013). Analysis: The potential and pitfalls of "big data" for humanitarians. Retrieved August 3, 2013, from http://www.irinnews.org/report/98104/analysis-potential-pitfalls-of-big-data-for-humanitarians

Nunn, N., & Qian, N. (2012, January). *Aiding conflict: The impact of U.S. food aid on civil war.* NBER Working Paper No. 17794. Retrieved June 20, 2013, from http://www.nber.org/papers/w17794.

OECD (Organisation for Economic Cooperation and Development). (2011, June 27). Press release.

Rome: UN. (1996). Rome declaration on world food security and world food summit plan of action. Retrieved July 24, 2013, from http://www.unglobalpulse.org/about-new

UN Global Pulse. (2014). Annual Report. Retrieved from http://www.unglobalpulse.org/sites/default/files/Annual%20Report_2014_FINAL-DIGITAL-FOR%20EMAIL_0.pdf

UN Office for the Coordination of Humanitarian Affairs. (2013). Hunger warning for Guinea-Bissau as cashew price dips. Retrieved July 18, 2013, from http://www.irinnews.org/report/98434/hunger-warning-for-guinea-bissau-as-cashew-price-dips

United Nations Food and Agriculture Organisation. (2012). *The state of food insecurity in the world 2012.* Rome: UN.

INDEX

© The Editor(s) (if applicable) and The Author(s) 2016   137
A. Bunnik et al. (eds.), *Big Data Challenges*,
DOI 10.1057/978-1-349-94885-7